"Adam Young has been a gift to us from Father
brought him into our li
our families of origin on
agement we received fr
to the Enneagram and o
deeply into *Make Sense o*
invaluable insights for every season of your journey."

Beth and Jeff McCord, founders of Your Enneagram Coach

"Adam Young has become one of my favorite people to learn from. He has a wonderful way of helping us look into the most sacred parts of our lives—our stories. *Make Sense of Your Story* has the power to lead us into the whole and healed life we all long for. To do this work requires much of us, but we have a trusted and incredibly skilled guide in Adam. I can't recommend this book enough."

Rich Villodas, pastor of New Life Fellowship and author of *The Narrow Path*

"With great care and baring of his soul, Adam digs deep into how stories shape spirit and cells. This is valuable information, unraveling myths and reweaving what is frayed, as intimate as across the table. For those whose stories feel fragmented, without anchor or lighthouse, Adam gently walks with you to do the difficult and needed work."

J. S. Park, hospital chaplain and author of *As Long As You Need: Permission to Grieve*

"Those of us who have grown up in communities and practices of faith are no strangers to stories. Unfortunately, most of those stories are about other people—leaving our inner worlds an unexplored mystery that shapes our present moment without our awareness. In this book, Young invites us to know our stories so that we can not only know ourselves but be in an embodied, aware, present relationship with ourselves and others. Young invites us to see that understanding our past supports us to engage more meaningfully with God, with hope, and with connection in our present and future."

Dr. Hillary McBride, registered psychologist, speaker, podcaster, and author of *The Wisdom Of Your Body*

"Nothing separates humans from other creatures quite so much as the fact that, at our core, we are storytellers. No wonder, then, that the anguish of our present age reflects the stories we tell ourselves about ourselves—the stories in which we believe we are living. What are we to do? In God's great mercy, in Adam Young we have a herald who comes to us with humility, vulnerability, and deep wisdom. And with *Make Sense of Your Story*, he offers us a gift that is a beautiful story itself, one that invites us to tell our own stories more truly—despite how difficult it may be to do so—by listening to and becoming part of the story God has been telling each of us from the beginning. If a story of greater beauty and goodness is one in which you long to live, by all means, read this book."

Curt Thompson, MD, author of *The Soul of Desire* and *The Deepest Place*

"In *Make Sense of Your Story*, Adam Young extends a life-altering invitation to take our story seriously. The challenge for many of us is that we have so few places to fully explore the complexities of our experiences—the stories in which desire, trauma, failure, and emptiness all vie for the right to shape our future. This is why Adam's debut book is so vital. He has a beautiful ability to weave together neuroscience, biblical wisdom, and storytelling, providing insights that leave us feeling not only more knowledgeable but deeply understood. This is a rare book that offers clarity for those who feel lost and profound kindness for those who are hurting."

Jay Stringer, psychotherapist and author of *Unwanted: How Sexual Brokenness Reveals Our Way to Healing*

"Adam's mind is a true gift, and he has an uncanny ability to bring complex concepts of psychology and theology to an accessible level where the reader can not only understand them but put them into practice to transform the way they engage their story. This book is a brilliant guide to understanding your past trauma, its impact in your life, and how to begin healing"

Cathy Loerzel, coauthor of *Redeeming Heartache* and cofounder of The Allender Center

"Adam Young's *Make Sense of Your Story* is a profound exploration of the transformative power of understanding one's personal narrative. It is not a book to rush through, as the journey of healing is intimate work that requires insight and kindness. Young masterfully guides us through the essential journey of making sense of our stories, particularly those rooted in our family of origin, to restore peace and relational wholeness in our lives, and he provides a compassionate framework for holistic healing of body and spirit. His skillful use of biblical narratives, cultural stories, and personal experience weaves an understanding of our essential need to be seen, heard, cherished, and reconnected. This book is an invaluable resource for anyone seeking to heal and transform their life story with grace and empathy."

J. Derek McNeil, president of The Seattle School of Theology & Psychology

MAKE SENSE OF
YOUR STORY

MAKE SENSE OF YOUR STORY

Why Engaging Your Past with Kindness Changes Everything

ADAM YOUNG

BakerBooks

a division of Baker Publishing Group
Grand Rapids, Michigan

© 2025 by Adam Young

Published by Baker Books
a division of Baker Publishing Group
Grand Rapids, Michigan
BakerBooks.com

Printed in the United States of America

All rights reserved. No part of this publication may be reproduced, stored in a retrieval system, or transmitted in any form or by any means—for example, electronic, photocopy, recording—without the prior written permission of the publisher. The only exception is brief quotations in printed reviews.

Library of Congress Cataloging-in-Publication Data
Names: Young, Adam, 1973– author.
Title: Make sense of your story : why engaging your past with kindness changes everything / Adam Young.
Description: Grand Rapids : Baker Books, a division of Baker Publishing Group, [2025] | Includes bibliographical references.
Identifiers: LCCN 2024022435 | ISBN 9781540903754 (paperback) | ISBN 9781540904690 (casebound) | ISBN 9781493449064 (ebook)
Subjects: LCSH: Autobiography—Religious aspects—Christianity. | Storytelling—Religious aspects—Christianity.
Classification: LCC BR1690 .Y78 2025 | DDC 248.4—dc23/eng/20240805
LC record available at https://lccn.loc.gov/2024022435

The names and details of the people and situations described in this book have been changed or presented in composite form in order to ensure the privacy of those with whom the author has worked.

Unless otherwise indicated, Scripture quotations are from the Holy Bible, New International Version®, NIV®. Copyright © 1973, 1978, 1984, 2011 by Biblica, Inc.® Used by permission of Zondervan. All rights reserved worldwide. www.zondervan.com. The "NIV" and "New International Version" are trademarks registered in the United States Patent and Trademark Office by Biblica, Inc.®

Scripture quotations labeled ESV are from The Holy Bible, English Standard Version® (ESV®). Copyright © 2001 by Crossway, a publishing ministry of Good News Publishers. Used by permission. All rights reserved. ESV Text Edition: 2016

Cover design by Faceout Studio, Jeff Miller

Published in association with The Bindery Agency, www.TheBinderyAgency.com.

Baker Publishing Group publications use paper produced from sustainable forestry practices and postconsumer waste whenever possible.

25 26 27 28 29 30 31   7 6 5 4 3 2 1

To Rick Wilson: when I was a lost high school kid who didn't know his right hand from his left, you loved me. *Your love changed my life.*

CONTENTS

Foreword by Dan Allender 11

1. Why Story Matters 15

2. What If Your Story Isn't in the Past? 35

3. Common Objections to Exploring Your Story 55

4. What If You Engaged Your Family of Origin Story? 67

5. Insecure Attachment: Avoidant and Ambivalent Attachment 93

6. Naming What Is Most True about Your Story 109

7. What If You Engaged Your Sexual Story? 127

8. What If You Listened to the Story Your Body Is Telling You? 159

9. What If You Explored Your Collective/Cultural Story? 179

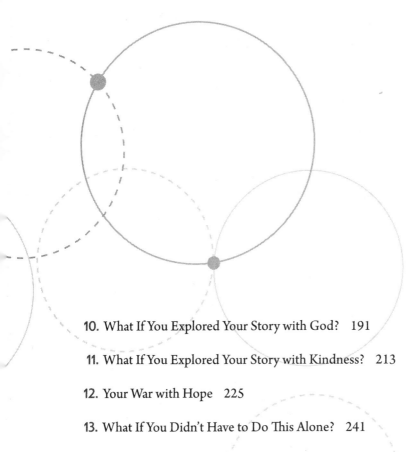

10. What If You Explored Your Story with God? 191

11. What If You Explored Your Story with Kindness? 213

12. Your War with Hope 225

13. What If You Didn't Have to Do This Alone? 241

  Acknowledgments 253

> Illusions mistaken for truth are the pavement under our feet. They are what we call civilization.
>
> Barbara Kingsolver, *The Poisonwood Bible*

FOREWORD

BY DAN ALLENDER

There is a story my mother often told me about how I got my name. She was an only child and deeply bound to her father, my grandfather. He was a famous veterinarian and bred and ran hunting dogs at various contests. She asked which name he wanted for his first grandson. He hated all his names and said, "Name him after my favorite dog: Comanche Dan." My name is neither Comanche nor Daniel. My name is Dan.

I never met my grandfather; he died before I was a year old. I have no proof the story is true other than that my grandmother, who lived until I was twenty-five, never contradicted its veracity. However, my mother was not fond of the truth, and my grandmother seldom stood in the way of my mother's pathology. I don't know if the story is true, but my mother wanted me to hear it often for some reason.

We are all a story within countless stories. We are like Russian Matryoshka dolls. If you open one story, another is nesting in the next, and no matter how many dolls or stories you open, there is another waiting for you to explore.

We are neither infinite nor anywise close, but all our stories, nesting in the heavens like the stars, eventually run back to Eden and the story of our foremother and father. We are brazenly finite, but our stories span the universe like the sands of the sea. The fact that we can't take them all in doesn't mean they don't exist. The reality is that just as we are made from the minerals of the stars through the big bang, we are also the children of Adam and Eve.

It is too much for us to fathom, and we are ineluctably drawn to explore our own story and all the stories of heaven and earth. We want to make sense of our story and the stories of those we love and hate. But too often, we do so in a way that offers an explanation bearing a finality and clarity that simply are not true.

I don't know if this origin story of my name is accurate. But I know that I heard it often. I will never know whether my mother created a fable, was dabbling in historical fiction, or told the utter truth. But it is necessary to ponder and reflect on what she wanted me to know in telling that story.

I am responsible for my story. I am not responsible for its veracity in ensuring every portion of what I remember or hear is factually accurate. We know only too well from research that our memory is a form of storytelling, and we leave out portions of what is too disconcerting or inconceivable until our body and heart are ready to receive new truths as a welcomed guest.

Tragically, many people will never welcome the unspoken, unremembered parts of their story that bear heartache and shame. Those parts remain in us, like stardust, whether we want to believe in the big bang or not. What we deny or ignore won't go away—it remains within us, calling us back so that we, in turn, might move forward. Our stories haunt us until we look underneath the bed and find there really are monsters to be slain and not just cobwebs or our imaginings.

What I love about Adam Young is his integrity; knowing that he doesn't want to look under the bed, he also knows he must. It is too easy to ask one's mother to peer under the bed and tell us there are no monsters. But what do we do with consolation from the one who is, in part, the monster we fear near our bed? As a child, all we can do is take whatever false comfort is available until we dare to look under the bed for ourselves.

Adam is a brilliant writer and therapist, but far more, he is a courageous adult/child. He holds the unfathomable in his hands and asks kind—deeply kind—questions that invite the fearful, shameful, and furious stories to come out from hiding and speak to us about our origin. His ability to speak to our fear and invite us as adults to care for our fragmented parts is holy and wise.

No matter how often or well you have considered your story, as I did, you will find a depth of goodness in letting Adam guide you in excavation and recovery. As much as I admire the clarity of the scaffolding provided, I cherish the honor and blessing Adam brings to the process even more. Without a doubt, you will not be the same person you were when you began the book, but who you discover yourself to be will be an even more excellent gift to those you love.

This glorious book is a love story, and you are the central figure on the stage. But embedded in this story is the God who wrote you, and as you open one story to the next, you will meet the One who made you, redeemed you, and invigorates you to live your story for the sake of love.

1

WHY STORY MATTERS

> The past is never dead; it's not even past.
> William Faulkner, *Requiem for a Nun*

I was six years old when I nervously dialed Mrs. Heidenreich's phone number. She was the mother of my friend who lived across the street. When she answered, I said "I love you" and hung up. My heart was pounding, but I had finally done it. I had told Mrs. Heidenreich that I loved her.

What kind of six-year-old does this? Why would I have done this?

Five years later, I was standing in a pool facing my mother. All of a sudden, I slapped her across the face. Hard. I had never come close to hitting my mother before that day, and I never came close to hitting her after that day. Why does an eleven-year-old with no history of violence suddenly slap his mother in a pool?

As a twenty-year-old, right after a family counseling session, I got into the car with my father, held his hand with interlocking fingers, and said, "Dad, I love you so much. I will always love you. I will love you more than my future wife." Why would a twenty-year-old make a pledge like this to his father?

When I was first introduced to the notion of story work as a thirty-five-year-old man, none of the above three stories registered as significant to me. I couldn't explain any of them—that is, I couldn't *make sense* of these stories—but it didn't matter to me because I felt no need to understand these odd incidents that were a seemingly very tiny part of my past life. They were simply offbeat anecdotes.

You probably have similar snippets of memories. There are pieces of stories you likely remember or would soon be able to remember if you flipped through a photo album. Perhaps you've dismissed most of these stories as irrelevant to your present life, just as I did. Whatever fragments of memories you may remember, please know this: more stories are there. Tucked in the recesses of your heart and mind. Waiting for you to explore them.

Shortly after that family counseling session when I was twenty, I found myself back at the College of William and Mary for my sophomore year. Ever since first arriving at college, I had been experiencing increasing levels of anxiety and depression. Emotional pain became a frequent companion. When it got bad enough, I'd put my Bible and a journal in my backpack and ride my bike to Lake Matoaka, a secluded lake at the edge of campus. I'd hike into the woods, find a private spot, and begin a familiar endeavor: voraciously reading the Bible, desperately looking for answers to my questions. *If Jesus loves me, why do I feel so much pain* so often? *What's wrong with me? Other people don't seem to be experiencing the anxiety and depression I feel; what are they doing that I'm not doing?*

At church and at InterVarsity Christian Fellowship, I was told Jesus was the person my heart was most looking for and most needed, and the Bible would help me to know Jesus. And so I'd go to Lake

Matoaka, desperately seeking Jesus and earnestly devouring the Bible, looking for help with my pain.

Fifteen years passed and little changed in my anguished heart. I had tried everything: books, conferences, mentors, Bible studies, journaling, prayer, counseling. I don't just mean a few books or a few meetings with mentors. I mean hundreds of books, several years of weekly meetings with mentors, and innumerable pages written in my journal. But more than any of these endeavors, I prayed and read the Bible. I would ask, seek, and knock—pleading with God for help. Over and over and over. Year in and year out for my entire twenties and well into my thirties. To say that I read the Bible doesn't really do it justice. I *studied* the Bible. Searching, searching, searching for the answers to my questions. *Why do I feel so empty and worthless one minute, and then anxious and panicky the next?*

By the time I was thirty-five I had done everything I knew to answer this simple question: How do I make it hurt less inside? How do I get well?

Around this time, someone gave me a copy of *The Wounded Heart* by Dan Allender. This was my introduction to story work.

It was my introduction to the idea that I had a story.

This book suggested that my story was not just something in my past but was also profoundly affecting how I experienced the world in the present. I thought to myself, *Maybe understanding my story can help me discover why I am in so much pain?*

What about you? You may have tried everything you know to find healing, to grow and mature.

But have you engaged your story?

Engaging your story means a lot more than writing down your life narrative and journaling or thinking about it. The Counting Crows' song "Round Here" is about a woman who considers jumping off a building, and one particular lyric moves me: "She says she's tired of life / She must be tired of something."[1]

Many of us are tired. Tired of *something*. What if most of your exhaustion is caused by running from your story? By this I simply mean ignoring how your past is affecting your present.

My goal with this book is to cultivate in you a deeper yearning to know and understand the most pivotal stories of your life. If the yearning is there, the story work will follow. Change begins in the gut.

I also hope to awaken in you the courage to deeply engage your life story.

The good news is that both of these—desire and courage—are already inside of you. How do I know that? Because you are created in the image of a God who has deep desire and great courage. You don't have to create either one. What if you took the desire and courage that are already inside of you and let them lead you on a journey of exploring your story more deeply?

Like me, you may have tried many things in your efforts to heal and grow. Sadly, it's very possible to read great books, attend helpful conferences, participate in Bible study groups—even do therapy with a decent therapist—and *still not engage your personal story in depth*.

Most books, Bible studies, and conferences focus on information transfer and lean heavily on the belief that right information leads to right living—full stop. Unfortunately, much counseling stops there as well. Information is not going to heal you; information is not going to catalyze growth and maturation in your heart and brain.

Many Bible studies are primarily cognitive experiences. If you put the people in your small group into fMRI machines while you were

---

1. Counting Crows, "Round Here," *August and Everything After* (Geffen Records, 1994).

having your Bible study, it is likely the thinking parts of your brains would be lit up but the parts devoted to emotions, bodily sensations, and autobiographical memory would be largely inactive. That is tragic. Jesus is interested in your *heart*, and all church communities should likewise touch your heart as well as stimulate your head. To engage your story is to collide with your heart.

My invitation to you is simple: take your story seriously. As seriously as God takes it.

Engaging your story is the single most important thing you can do to experience healing.

Exploring your story will take you further into healing and growth than traditional talk therapy, which often allows you to remain safely disconnected from the parts of you that hold deep feelings, unmet longings, and disturbing bodily sensations. However, if you start to talk about particular scenes from your story, you will soon start to feel deep feelings, connect with unmet longings, and experience important bodily sensations. In other words, you will connect to your limbic brain and therefore to a storehouse of implicit memories (more about this soon).

This is where you need to be to experience deeper healing and growth.

It's easy to berate yourself for what you imagine is wrong with you. *But what if every symptom you have makes sense and is telling a story?*

More importantly, what if every symptom you have points back to a story—a story that has something vital to reveal to you?

There was a reason I was feeling so much anxiety in college. There was a reason I felt like there was something wrong with me. Likewise, there is a reason for your symptoms—whatever they are. There is a reason your life is the way it is. There is a reason you are stuck in the places where you are stuck. And that reason will be found by exploring your story, particularly your story in your family of origin.

WHO IS THIS BOOK FOR?

This book is for those of us who have difficulties with relationships, difficulties with emotions, and/or difficulties with God. We are also people who often have a difficult time being inside our own bodies.

Do you have a sense that your insides are not quite right? That something is off? Please consider the possibility that this does *not* mean there is something wrong with you. On the contrary, this may simply mean you are paying attention. There is a part of you that is *awake*—and aware that the status quo is not the way things are supposed to be.

Difficulties with Relationships

How are you supposed to know if you have difficulties with relationships? To begin with, think about how you navigate conflict, or "rupture and repair."

Rupture refers to any relational interaction that leaves you with a felt sense of disconnection from the other person. It's painful. *Repair* refers to engaging the conflict in a way where both people feel heard, understood, and validated, and the relational connection is restored.

The fact that we live in a sinful world means that relational rupture is inevitable and frequent: you will do harm, and you will be harmed by others.

You may be asking, "What if I don't have conflict in my relationships?"

If your relationships never rupture, it does not mean you are spiritually and emotionally mature. It means you are refusing to honestly share your full self (your true thoughts, feelings, and longings) with the other person. In short, it means you are compromising your integrity for the sake of some morsel of relational connection and belonging. But if this is you—if you are realizing you sometimes compromise your integrity for the sake of belonging—this does not mean you are a bad person.

It just means you have a story. There is a reason you do the things you do.

The mark of spiritual health and emotional maturity is the ability to move through the process of rupture and repair on a regular basis—with integrity. *Integrity* means that you do not swallow your true thoughts, feelings, and desires to avoid conflict or to prematurely "restore" the relational rupture.

Think about your relationships for a minute. In which relationships do you feel free to express your true thoughts, feelings, and longings? In which relationships do you feel the need to edit yourself? Where are you not bringing the fullness of who you are or what you want or where you're disappointed . . . because you don't want to disrupt the status quo of the relationship?

Each of us relates to other people in the style we do because of our story! There is a reason we show up relationally the way we do. Difficulties with relationships often indicate an unexamined, unhealed story. If you have difficulties with relationships, this book will help you understand why.

Difficulties with Emotions

Many people think that saying "I have difficulties with emotions" is synonymous with "I have trouble keeping my emotions under control." Nothing could be further from the truth. Your emotions are not supposed to be kept under control. They are not supposed to be kept under anything. Emotions are designed by God to move you. This truth is right there in the word itself. E-motions are intended to put your body *into motion* (to evoke motion). Each one of your emotions is an authentic and meaningful response to what is happening inside or outside of you (or both). Your emotions are truth-tellers that are constantly sending signals—they are not meant to be controlled but rather listened to.

Neuroscientist Dan Siegel says we are hardwired to connect to one another, and the way we do so is through emotions.[2]

For example, sadness is intended to prompt you to move your body toward another for comfort and support. Anger is intended to prompt you to move your body toward another to address something that is not right. Joy is intended to prompt you to move your body toward another for the purpose of heightened, shared delight. Fear is intended to prompt you to move your body away from danger and toward the safety found in being protected by another.

The point is that emotions should lead you to *move your body*. If you are trying to keep your emotions under control, you are working against God's purpose for giving you emotions.

So, what does it mean to have difficulty with emotions? It means that you have trouble feeling all your emotions deeply *and* you have trouble expressing them in a way that builds up or benefits yourself and those around you. If you have difficulties with emotions, this book will help you understand why.

Difficulties with God

God is the coauthor of our stories. For me, this reality is both relieving and agonizing. It's relieving because it brings me hope that my story is not over and that the Creator of all beauty may create a beautiful ending to my story. It's agonizing because it begs the question, Why didn't God protect me from so much trauma and abuse?

If you're honest, you know that you carry anger at God inside of you. And, perhaps more difficult to address, you carry *disappointment* with God inside of you.

---

2. Daniel Siegel, Diana Fosha, and Marion Solomon, eds., *The Healing Power of Emotion: Affective Neuroscience, Development & Clinical Practice*, Norton Series on Interpersonal Neurobiology (New York: W. W. Norton, 2009), vii.

What have you done with your anger at God and your disappointment in God?

To say it differently, Where are you unwilling to bring your full self to God? In what ways do you edit the questions of your heart? Where are you trying to numb yourself so that you don't have to talk to God about your disappointment?

More than anything, most of us yearn for God's comfort. We want to know a God who is willing to get into the fire with us and transform our stories of pain and confusion into stories of redemption and healing.

If you have difficulties with God, this book is for you.

The Holiness of Discontent

This book is also for people who have a holy discontent with the way things are in the modern world. People who want more out of life.

Contemporary life for many people includes a profound lack of community (significant isolation and separation from others), as well as a profound lack of meaning. Are you dissatisfied with your lack of connectedness to other people? Do you feel like you are just going through the motions and doing what your culture says you should do? There is a reason you feel isolated, and there is a reason you would like to feel a deeper sense of meaning in your life.

There is a reason you have a holy discontent with the way things are for you. *And that reason is rooted in your story.* Don't assume there is something wrong with you because you feel disappointed with your level of connection to others and lack of meaning in your life. You were created for deep relational connection. You were also created to live a meaningful life and to have a significant impact in your corner of the world, no matter how small.

WHAT WE WANT

The biblical word for what we all want is *shalom*. Shalom refers to "the webbing together of God, humans, and all creation in justice, fulfillment, and delight."[3] Human beings are designed by God to experience shalom, which happens when you have peace, harmony, and delight between:

You and you.

You and other people.

You and the earth.

You and your Creator.

When the various regions of your brain and body are well connected (integrated), you experience intrapersonal shalom (you and you). When you are meaningfully connected with the important people in your life, you experience interpersonal shalom (you and other people). When you are in a connected, harmonious relationship with the earth, you experience shalom with the land. When you are meaningfully connected to your Creator, you experience shalom with God.

When these four elements of connection are in place, you experience fullness of life. This is the way it's supposed to be. The Bible calls this peace, harmony, and delight *shalom*; interpersonal neurobiologists call it *integration*. But it's the same thing. *It's what we all want*. It's what we were all created for.

There is a way to move from disconnection to connection in these four areas. There is a way to experience more shalom within yourself. There is a way to experience more shalom between you and other people. There is a way to experience more shalom with the earth. And there is a way to experience more shalom with God.

---

3. Cornelius Plantinga, *Not the Way It's Supposed to Be: A Breviary of Sin* (Grand Rapids: Eerdmans, 1996), 10.

How? The starting point is simply this: you have to make sense of your story, especially your story in your family of origin.

WHAT I MEAN BY "YOUR STORY"

For years, I didn't think I had a story. I certainly had no notion that my past story was influencing my present day-to-day life. You may not think of your past story as significant, but you would be wrong. It is massively significant. More than any other single factor, your past story is responsible for the way your brain operates today. But what exactly is "your story"?

Your story refers to the experiences you've had in life, particularly in your family of origin. When most people think of their life story, they think of an overarching narrative of their life from birth until eighteen, usually from a bird's-eye view. If you were thirty thousand feet up in the air looking down on your town, you could accurately describe what you see, but your description wouldn't be very detailed.

Many people tell their story from this distant perspective. For example, I could say, "My dad was a workaholic and didn't spend much time with me or my brothers. When he wasn't working, he was outside with his plants. I was much closer to my mom than my dad. I got good grades in school to earn my dad's approval but it never got me what I really wanted—a father who was involved in my life." That thirty-thousand-foot recounting of my life is true but also merely objective facts—it's not what I mean by "your story."

Your story is far more about the individual scenes you still remember from your growing-up years.

> That day on the soccer field in third grade.
>
> That time your mom finally stood up to your dad.

> That time you forgot about a school assignment and asked your mom to get you poster board, and when she left the house your dad lost his temper and hit you.

When you recount a particular individual scene, you are telling a story at ground level rather than from thirty thousand feet.

If I only had two hours to work with you, I would much rather hear you tell one story at ground level than your overarching life narrative. Why? Because *trauma resides in the details*.

It doesn't reside in the big picture. When you offer a thirty-thousand-foot telling of your story, you are able to remain comfortably distant from the big emotions you would feel if you told just one of your stories at ground level.

In fact, you don't really have "a story." You have *stories*. Lots of them.

Together, they make up your overarching life story. The illuminating evidence is really found in the individual stories, the particular scenes.

When you offer a distant telling of your story, it's usually a cover-up. You're not lying, you're just omitting the details of the events that have wounded you. But when you offer a ground-level telling of a particular moment, the crime scene comes into sharp focus.

> The time your dad was drunk at your eleventh birthday party and said that cruel thing to you, and you were humiliated in front of your friends.

> The time your younger brother tracked mud through the house and your dad violently spanked him while you stood in the doorway of your room, helplessly watching and hearing your brother scream.

What are one or two of the individual scenes you remember?

A good story has a variety of settings, characters, plotlines, and themes. The story of your life is no different.

Settings

Think of all the settings that compose your life story: your kindergarten class, the first soccer team you played on, your piano recital when you were ten years old, junior prom, the room in your house where that really bad thing happened that your family never talks about.

Characters

Then there are all the characters who make an appearance in the epic story that is your life:

> Your parents, siblings, grandparents, uncles and aunts, and cousins.
> Your second grade teacher, your basketball coach, your violin instructor, the neighbor kids who lived down the street.
> Your first boyfriend or girlfriend.

And if you moved to a new place when you were a kid, a whole new cast of characters entered your story. Have you ever written down the important characters in your life? Just listed them on a piece of paper? Try it. And then look at that piece of paper and realize how epic your life story really is.

We tend to focus on the characters who were always there. However, what about the characters who entered your story for a short season but played an important role? Did you have a teacher who cared deeply for you during a particularly hard season of your life? For example, Rick Wilson was my Young Life leader for three years in high school. Relatively speaking, we spent very little time together.

But Rick loved me. *And I knew it.*

His impact on my heart was incalculable. I've had virtually no contact with him since I graduated from high school, but when I think about the people in my life who've truly loved me, his name is at the top of the list.

Finally, there are the characters in your story who should have played a much more significant role but were largely absent. Don't underestimate absence. One of the biggest "characters" in your story may be the absence of someone you needed.

Plotlines

In addition to all the characters who make an appearance in your story, you also have innumerable plotlines holding your story together. Just think how varied they are!

There's the plotline of your relationship with your father. What are the pivotal points in your relationship with him? What *moments* made that relationship what it was in the past and what it is today? What conversations? What incidents?

There are moments seemingly frozen in time that we remember. When I was playing soccer as a third grader, my dad would sometimes come to my games. He wouldn't stand with the other parents. I played center forward, so my dad would stand at the top of the opposing team's penalty box. When I would get the ball and dribble toward the goal, my dad would yell "Strike it!" and it was like everything else went silent. The cheering parents, the other kids yelling, the sound of an airplane overhead ... it was all completely silent. All I could hear was my dad's voice. This little snippet of a memory tells you volumes about the story of my relationship with my dad.

What is the plotline of your relationship with your mom? If you were to storyboard your relationship with her but could only include one scene for each year of your life, which scenes would make the cut?

Then there's the plotline of your love life—all the people you dated. Or didn't date. If you are married, your marriage has a story. If you never married, one of your plotlines involves what it has been like to be single in a world that privileges married people. If you are divorced, there is the plotline of the devastation (and/or release) from your previous marriage ... and the war with hope as you consider risking marriage again.

One fundamental plotline of your story pertains to what you have done with your *desires* and your *disappointments*.

If I asked you to write your life story solely through the lens of desire—desires met and unmet—what would the chapter titles be? What are your top five fulfilled desires? Top five unfulfilled desires? The most agonizing and fulfilling plotlines of your story are those concerning your desires and disappointments.

I am much more interested in the deep desires of your heart than I am in what you have accomplished. I don't want to minimize your accomplishments—they matter—but they're not what is most beautiful about your story.

Tell me about your longings; tell me about what you wanted when you were fourteen. And why you wanted it. Then I will know something about the beauty of who you really are.

And then there are your disappointments. What are the disappointments that have leveled you? These, too, speak volumes about your heart—who you are and what matters to you.

The depth of your disappointment is directly related to the immensity of your longing and the robustness of your hope. In other words, your felt agony of disappointment will be greatest if you really, really want something *and* you let yourself actually hope that you will get it. It is the combination of deep longing plus risking hope that makes disappointment so devastating.

Another pivotal plotline in your story pertains to your relationship with God. The core story of your heart is the story of how you have interacted with God about your desires and disappointments. Even if you don't believe in God, when you don't get something you really want, there is a felt sense that the cosmos has let you down.

If you do believe in God, what happens inside your body when you risk longing for something and you risk hoping for something . . . and it doesn't happen?

Your fiancée breaks off the engagement. Your boss passes over you for the promotion. Someone else is chosen to lead the group you really wanted to lead. Disappointments leave a mark.

The way you respond to a particular disappointment often sets the trajectory for the next phase of your life. Please don't hear this as "Strong people bounce back from disappointments." Ugh. That is not what I'm saying.

My point is this: if you are going to understand why your story has unfolded the way it has, you have to look at how you responded to your disappointments.

How do you talk to God or engage with God after you have been disappointed?

Ultimately, all disappointments implicate God, the One who could have intervened and didn't. If you look up the etymology of the word *disappointment*, you will find that it originally meant "to miss an appointment with someone." A "dis-appointment" is a broken appointment.

All disappointment carries with it the sense of a broken appointment with God: you expected God to show up, and God didn't. *God could have let me get into that college and didn't. God didn't show up for me. God could have prevented that illness and didn't. God didn't show up.*

You cannot know yourself until you have been willing to name the deepest longings of your heart and the most devastating disappointments of your life.

More than anything else, your desires and disappointments reveal *who you are as a person*. More than your Enneagram number, Myers-Briggs type, or any other personality instrument.

To understand the unique way in which you reflect the glory of God—the thing that makes you *you*—it's important to name what you really want and what has broken your heart.

Most of our disappointments are ultimately about belonging... or not belonging. As relational beings created in the image of a triune Relationship, we were *built to belong.* Yet many of us have unmet longings around belongingness. *Where are* my *people? Why can't I find a small community (a few people even!) where I can actually be my full self and be fully embraced?* That's belonging.

Your life story has a number of plot twists, just like all great stories. A story without plot twists is not even a story. By "plot twist" I mean that you are headed in a particular direction and have energy toward that end and then *Bam!* Something happens, and your trajectory is abruptly changed.

All plot twists result in some measure of disorientation. It is in seasons of disorientation that we find out what we actually desire and what we're really made of. When you tell me how you have responded to the plot twists in your life story, I will learn a lot about your character.

Themes

Last, over the course of your life, themes emerge. You may not be able to see them yet, but they are developing. The theme of powerlessness. The theme of betrayal. The theme of how you have been repeatedly envied.

Here's the point: your life story is far more epic than Hollywood's best offerings. It has more diverse settings, more significant characters, thicker plotlines, and more intriguing, well-developed themes.

But why does your past story matter *now?* You may be thinking, *Okay, so I have a story. How does that affect my present life? What's the big deal?*

The big deal is that your stories have shaped your brain more than anything else. Which means that your stories are shaping your present day-to-day life far more than you realize.

WHY YOUR STORY MATTERS

You have an organ that is encased by your skull. It's called your brain. How did your brain come to be what it is? Unlike your other organs—kidneys, liver, stomach—your brain has changed massively as your story has unfolded. Why? Your kidneys haven't changed that much. Why has your brain?

Your brain is composed of billions of neurons. Each individual neuron is connected to thousands of other neurons. When neurons connect to one another, they form *neural networks*.

There are only two ways neural networks develop: through genetics and through life experiences.

So, when I speak of "your stories," I am speaking of your brain. With the exception of the genes that were passed on to you, the composition of your brain is entirely a function of *the experiences you have had in life*.

Said another way, excluding the genes you were born with, the structure of your brain is entirely a function of your stories!

If your brain has primarily developed in response to your stories, don't you think it might be important to become an expert on those stories? Understanding your stories will allow you to know why your brain has been shaped the way it has, which will allow you to understand why you experience your day-to-day life the way you do.

This is an oversimplification, but it goes basically like this: whenever you have an experience in the present, the first thing your brain does is filter that experience through all your past experiences. That's how brains operate. That's what neural networks do.

Many people want to experience change and to grow as human beings. Good. Here's the dilemma: you are not going to experience meaningful, heart-level change until you engage your stories. Why? Because *change* means that neurons link up differently with one another. Change means there is a shift in how the neurons in your brain connect with one another.

You are not going to change deeply until you engage your neurons . . . which means until you engage the experiences you have had in life.

Which is to say, your stories.

CHAPTER 1 KEY POINTS

- Human beings are designed to experience shalom—peace, harmony, and delight—with self, with others, with the earth, and with God.
- There is a way to restore shalom to your body: the starting point is to make sense of your story, particularly your story in your family of origin.
- When I say "your story," I'm talking about the individual scenes, not the overarching narrative of your life.
- With the exception of the genes that were passed on to you, the composition of your brain is entirely a function of the experiences you have had in life.

2

WHAT IF YOUR STORY ISN'T IN THE PAST?

> Our stories become blueprints for our future.
> Louis Cozolino, *Why Therapy Works*

There is a link between your past stories and the way you are presently living your life. Isaiah 61:1 identifies this linkage:

> The Spirit of the Sovereign LORD is on me,
>   because the LORD has anointed me
> to proclaim good news to the poor.
> He has sent me to bind up the brokenhearted,
>   to proclaim freedom for the captives
>   and release from darkness for the prisoners.

When Isaiah says, "He has sent me to bind up the brokenhearted, to proclaim freedom for the captives," he is making a connection between being brokenhearted and becoming a captive.

Here's the connection: when your heart is wounded—when something breaks inside of you—you begin living in a way that promises to relieve the wound and assures you that you will never be hurt in that particular way again. And this way of living *enslaves you*. You become captive to it.

The captives and prisoners Isaiah speaks about so tenderly are precisely those people who have first had their hearts broken.

Some years ago I heard a man give a talk about one of his wounds. When he was in fifth grade, he was significantly overweight and had a thirty-six-inch waist. He tried to compensate for this by becoming the class clown. And it worked for a time. But one day the whole class had to do pull-ups for one of those national physical fitness tests.

Narrating the story of that day, his voice cracked as he said, "I couldn't pull myself up. I just hung there, utterly humiliated in front of all my classmates. As I hung there, I thought to myself, *I am so weak. I am not a boy. And I will never be a man.*"

That night he went home and decided he was never going to be humiliated like that again. He went for a run; four houses was as far as he could go. Yet for the next three years he didn't miss a single day of running. He went down to a twenty-nine-inch waist. But he also became anorexic and obsessive about exercise.

His wound led to captivity. His brokenheartedness resulted in becoming a prisoner to excessive exercise and an eating disorder.

This progression happens for each of us.

Our hearts are injured because of the sinfulness of other people in the world. And then we become captive to whatever ways we devise to protect ourselves from future harm.

This man was humiliated by his body; he became captive to living in such a way that he would never be humiliated by his body again. Does he need to repent of that way of living? Sure—but far more he needs healing for his broken heart. He needs healing of the wound that began as he hung from that pull-up bar, utterly humiliated as he agreed with evil that he was weak and would never be a man.

He needs to be set free from his captivity to exercising obsessively, hating his body, and punishing his body so that it will be strong enough to save him from future humiliation.

We become captive to those things that promise to protect our hearts from being wounded in the same way again. The Bible calls this idolatry.

Isaiah's claim is that *your idolatry grows in the soil of your pain.*

Your idolatry is not random.

There is a linkage between your captivity (idolatry) and how your heart has been broken. Your idolatry is deeply related to the experiences that have caused your brokenheartedness. In this way, your past story is profoundly influencing how you are presently living your life. Your past stories of harm (brokenheartedness) are deeply affecting your present life (the places where you are bound).

There is a reason you are captive to financial security . . . and that reason will be found in the story of how you've been wounded. Maybe you never felt safe in your house—never felt in control—and now the only way to feel safe is to make sure you have enough money in the bank.

There is a reason you are captive to such a high level of achievement that you are never able to rest . . . and that reason will be found in your story. Maybe your dad's approval was just out of reach—you got close to earning it, but not quite. And now you can't stop working and don't know why.

There is a reason you continue to find yourself in nonreciprocal friendships—that is, friendships in which you are always giving and rarely receiving. Perhaps your role in your family of origin was to give, give, give to your very needy mother.

There is always a story behind this stuff. And it's the story of the particular ways your heart has been wounded.

My dad was a marine, a Vietnam vet with full-blown post-traumatic stress disorder (PTSD). His platoon began with forty-eight men. Only twelve made it home. He had significant survivor's guilt and uncontrollable rage. He frequently lost his temper with me. I lived in terror of my father. Looking back, I now know he was terrified of himself. He would get enraged due to his trauma and take his rage out on his five-year-old son. When he screamed at me to pull my pants down for a "spanking," I would immediately comply, but as he raised his hand, I would always plead with him, saying "Just let me say one thing. Just let me say one thing."

As a five-year-old, I was pleading with my father to hear my side of the story. I needed my dad to understand why I didn't deserve to be hit. I needed him to understand that I wasn't bad. Dad would yell, "What?" and I would make my case. It never worked. The beating always came.

As a result, *powerlessness* began to fill the cells of my body. I was powerless to make my dad stop abusing me. But, worse than that, I was powerless to convince my dad that I wasn't bad and that I didn't deserve his rage.

Here's the point: my heart was broken by my dad's contempt, humiliation, and violence. And that brokenheartedness led to captivity because our idols grow in the soil of our pain.

What was my captivity? To begin with, that five-year-old boy became fiercely committed to never being humiliated again. Fiercely committed to never being powerless again.

And when I say "fiercely committed," I mean that I made a vow in the depth of my being: *I will never be in a powerless position again.* As children, we make commitments—vows—frequently. Vows are like unspoken verbal contracts with ourselves and with the universe.

They lead to a particular way of relating to other people, a particular way of being in the world. There is a reason you relate to other people in the style you do. There is a reason you have the "personality" you do. And those reasons are found in the particular stories of heartache and harm that make up your life story ... and the commitments/vows you made in the immediate wake of being deeply harmed.

What if your past experiences of heartache can help you understand why you are the way you are today? What if the wounds you experienced growing up hold the key to understanding the way you think, feel, and act now?

According to Jesus, it is the truth that will set you free (see John 8:32). Freedom can't come without truth, without honesty, without eyes wide open to what has actually happened to you on planet Earth. And that includes eyes wide open to the ways you have been harmed, even by—especially by—your family.

The world we inhabit is not as it should be. I think that's a rather uncontroversial statement. In biblical language, we live in a world marred by sin. And because of that, we have all been wounded by the sin of others.

I imagine you likely agree that we live in a sinful world, a world of harm. But how many examples can you give of how the sinfulness of the world has marred you, how the sinfulness of others has cut into your heart? What are the moments, the incidents, the stories in which your heart has been broken by the sin of others? Where has the shrapnel of this world lodged in your body?

Are you willing to name your sin—your failures—but have a hard time naming the ways you have been sinned against? Are you willing to confess how you have hurt another person (spouse, child, colleague) but have a much harder time naming how another person has hurt you? The invitation to explore your story is an invitation to consider how the harm of others has affected you.

WHY DO I HARM OTHERS THE WAY I DO?

Another linkage between your past and your present can be seen in what I've often heard Dan Allender call "the debris of your life," which refers to the ways you are harming other people.

It's important to know that everyone does harm. Everyone. The question is, *Why* do you harm others in the *particular* ways you do? You cannot robustly answer this question without identifying how your heart has been broken and how your behaviors have the capacity to break others as a result.

Your wounds are one reason you are hurting people right now in the particular ways you are doing so. You will continue to consciously and unconsciously hurt other people until you address how your heart has been wounded. It's inevitable.

There is a reason you blow up at your partner the way you do. *It's not random.* It's not that you had a bad day. No; something happened between the two of you that triggered one of your wounds, and your body reacted in anger.

Let me give a personal example from the debris of my life.

My wife, Caroline, often expresses an unmet longing for me to pursue her heart by asking her about her day and how she is doing. She longs for more "short, connecting conversations" that show I care about her and am interested in her, and that she matters to me. A reasonable request from a spouse.

Caroline has repeatedly expressed this unmet desire to me over many, many years. My internal response to her request has always been: *Of course she wants that. I'm glad she wants that. What's going on that I don't do more of that in our relationship? After all, I do that sort of thing for a living.* She wants me to listen to her and pursue her heart—that's what I do all day long as a therapist! How is it that my own wife does not benefit from my gifting? It's like a gourmet chef refusing to cook amazing meals for his wife. It begs the question, What's going on?

Each time Caroline brings up this topic in marriage counseling, I feel confusion about why I don't pursue her heart more and anger at myself for not fulfilling this very reasonable request.

When a behavior in the present doesn't make sense, it is usually because we don't understand how that behavior is rooted in the past.

If you are perplexed by why you feel or act in a particular way, it might be a good idea to ask yourself, *How might my present emotions or actions make sense in light of my story?* The key to making sense of your present life is to look at the pivotal experiences from your past that have shaped the neurons in your brain.

We have to look at my past story to understand my present behavior with my wife.

One day, as I pondered why I continued to fail at meeting Caroline's desire for care and pursuit, I found myself writing this in my journal:

> I hated being attuned to my mom all the time. I hated that I was required to pursue Mom's heart and ask her questions about her day when I got home from school. However, now, as an adult, I love pursuing people's hearts (I do it all day long as a therapist). *Except for my wife.* Why is my wife the one person who does not receive my attunement and attention and care? I think I know why ... because it would feel way too similar to how I was constantly required to attune to my mom and tend to her.

It might be helpful to know that one of the (unconscious) reasons I married Caroline was because I sensed she was emotionally self-sufficient—that is, she wouldn't require me to attune to her and tend to her and do all the things for her I was required to do for my mom as a boy.

I didn't marry Caroline to have to continue my role with Mom— constant attunement and engagement.

I married her because she didn't seem to need that from me; she didn't seem to require that of me. The feeling inside me was,

"Finally, I'm free. Finally, I can be done with the job of taking care of *the woman*."

I can bless that I am sick and tired of attuning to and tending to my mother. A child should never be asked to do that for a parent. I can bless my defiant stance of, "I am never doing that again." However, I love attuning to and pursuing my clients—many of whom are women. Clearly, my defiant stance does not apply to women in general. Why is my wife the only woman I don't want to care for?

Because my relationship with my wife *feels* very similar to my relationship with my mother. My relationship with my wife activates my implicit memory of what it felt like to be a boy who was required to be a husband to his mother.

It took me many years of hindsight to understand this, but my mom profoundly sexualized our relationship. A hug from her was never pure. The hug was never for me. It was for her. There was always a sense that something was being taken from me.

Here's the point: I can attune to female *clients* with no problem because I'm not in a sexual relationship with them. Therefore, those relationships don't *feel like* my relationship with my mom. Those relationships don't activate my felt bodily sense of what it was like to be hugged by my mom, or to be required to ask her how she was feeling, or to say encouraging things to buoy up Mom's fragile insides.

The ways I presently harm my wife are rooted in *the past story of my relationship with my mother*.

"Trying harder" to pursue Caroline's heart is never going to work. What is required is a robust repentance—which is to say, I have to engage the story of my relationship with my mom. I have to name the war I feel when I tend to my wife's heart. I have to grieve and rage over the ways my mother harmed me and set me up to be able to care wonderfully for every woman on the planet except the one who is most important to me!

Repentance that does not involve emotional engagement with your story is anemic and insufficient.

It will never result in true neuronal change (which is to say, change in what is commonly referred to as "the heart"). Until I explore the story of my relationship to my mother, I will not be able to meaningfully repent of my idolatrous ways of relating to my wife.

You might imagine—correctly—that I have been "trying really hard" to attune to my wife and to pursue her. Trying really hard for years. What have you been "trying really hard" to change in your life? The answer to this question will help you name where you are *stuck*. Let the "stuck places" in your life serve as diagnostic indicators of where your past story is influencing your present life.

What if the difficulties between you and your loved ones can best be understood by looking at your story? What if *there's a reason* you've been arguing with your partner about the same thing for twenty years? It's not because you're a bad person or your partner is a bad person—it's because you each have a story. And that past story is playing out in your present ways of relating to each other.

WHY SHOULD I ENGAGE MY STORY?

If you want to breathe again, live well, and become fully yourself, you will need to engage the pivotal stories from your past. That is the core invitation of this book. Here are four reasons to explore your stories in more depth:

1. Your past stories affect your brain—and therefore your present life—more than anything else.
2. Your captivities (the places you are bound) are directly linked to the particular ways you have been wounded in the past.
3. Your unaddressed wounds are one of the primary reasons you hurt other people in your life.

4. You can't repent in a meaningful, robust way until you identify how your idolatry/captivity is linked to how your heart has been broken.

Exploring your story will not be easy. It will likely stir up big feelings—feelings your body has been holding for years. It can be painful to remember what was true. You are allowed to go at your own pace. In fact, a posture of gentleness and patient curiosity will take you much further than a posture of "ripping the Band-Aid off."

WHAT IF MY STORY ISN'T THAT BAD?

Last year a woman came up to me after a talk I gave and said,

> "I'm intrigued by what you're saying about exploring your story, but I didn't experience anything traumatic growing up. I know people who have experienced real trauma, and those things didn't happen to me. I was raised in a good home with loving parents. However, something is not right inside of me. And, to make matters worse, I don't think I should feel this much pain since nothing that bad ever happened to me. *I don't feel like I have a right to be as messed up as I am.*"

This sentiment is not uncommon. But it is crazy-making. It's bad enough to feel emotional pain inside; however, emotional pain becomes agonizing when you don't feel like you have the right to feel it in the first place.

Trauma is pervasive and sin has ravaged this world; nevertheless, many people have this sense of "My story isn't that bad."

In Jeremiah 6:13–14 and again in 8:10–11, the Lord indicts the leadership of Israel for deceit. God says, twice:

> Prophets and priests alike,
>   all practice deceit.

> They dress the wound of my people
>> as though it were not serious.
> "Peace, peace," they say,
>> when there is no peace.

God was saying that the leadership of Israel—the prophets and priests—practiced deceit. *Deceit* refers to misleading someone by concealing the truth. How were the leaders concealing the truth? They were refusing to take the wounds of the people seriously. They were saying, "Peace, peace"—"Everything's fine"—when everything was not fine.

Sadly, *this is what many of us do with our own wounds.*

We are like the leaders of Israel—we do not take our wounds seriously. We deceive ourselves into believing that everything is fine when everything is not fine. "Peace, peace," we say—when there is no peace in our bodies. We have symptoms: anxieties, fears, depression, rage, relationship problems, problems with God—there are so many ways in which our bodies are saying "It is not well with me." We dress our wounds as though they are not serious.

Most of us have at least fragments of memory about painful things that happened during our growing-up years. But instead of being curious about how these wounds may still be affecting us, we say things like "That happened thirty years ago; I should be over it by now," or "That happened when I was in elementary school; I really don't think it's affecting me today."

It is very common to believe your story isn't "that bad." But notice something: the reason you hold this position is because you are comparing your story to the stories of others who (you believe) had it worse than you. Why would you compare your story to another person's story?

And what if comparing your story to another person's story serves to prevent you from exploring *your* story?

If your friend has two broken legs, it doesn't make your broken arm hurt any less. Why would you ignore your broken arm simply because your friend has a more severe wound?

Anytime you say "My story isn't that bad," you are *minimizing your wounds*. You are dressing your wounds as though they are not serious. "Peace, peace"—you're saying—"everything is fine," when everything is not fine.

Believe it or not, your parents were—and are—sinful people. This does not mean your parents are bad people, it simply means they are human like you. It also means, however, that you were raised by caregivers who harmed you to some degree.

I understand it can be very difficult to look at how your primary caregivers—who provided so much goodness—also did harm. There is something deeply disorienting about coming to see one's parents as flawed human beings. I am not asking you to ignore their goodness. To be honest about your parents is to be willing to name *both* their deep goodness and their failures. However, in my experience, most people are inclined to focus only on the good things and ignore the ways their parents did harm.

How did your mother's sin wound you? How did your father's sin affect you? Because they did. That's simply the consequence of being raised by someone other than Jesus.

As Dr. Larry Crabb pointed out decades ago, "Sin is a bigger problem than we think."[1] In other words, sin does damage. Sometimes that damage is severe and sometimes it is slight. But sin cuts into the heart.

When your father harms you severely, it's like a grenade goes off and shrapnel lodges in your body. If you don't attend to that shrapnel and gently dig it out, your body cannot heal. Alternatively, when your father harms you slightly, it's like a splinter embeds in the ball of your foot. The splinter may be small, but it can change the way

---

1. Larry Crabb, *Inside Out*, 25th anniversary ed. (Colorado Springs: NavPress, 2013), 91.

you walk. The point is that all past harms—both large and small—affect your present life.

If you are committed to the narrative of "My story isn't that bad / I had a good childhood / Nothing that bad ever happened to me," it may be because you are *minimizing* your story.

In fact, it is almost guaranteed that you are minimizing your story. How can I say this even though I don't know you? Because I can't think of a single person who has come into my office and done the opposite—someone who believed their story was affecting them *more* than it actually was.

Minimizing means dismissing or discounting how significantly your growing-up years have shaped the neurons that filter every experience you will have today. It means you don't really believe your story as a boy or a girl continues to profoundly affect your thoughts, feelings, and choices today. Everyone I know minimizes their story. Including me.[2]

Minimizing might look like this: your friend is sharing a painful story with you when she stops and says, "But I shouldn't complain . . . look at so-and-so, who is struggling with so much more adversity than me."

Another example: as you are reflecting back on some of the ways your mom hurt you, you catch yourself thinking, *But my mom had a bad childhood, far worse than mine. So I shouldn't be hurt from my childhood.*

Or, at a men's retreat, everyone is asked to share a story of harm from their childhood. One participant responds by saying, "When I think back on my childhood, I don't really have any harmful moments. I mean my parents got divorced when I was eleven, but it wasn't that bad. I remember having to tell my mom that my dad was having an

---

2. The antidote to minimizing your story is the experience of other people's *voices and faces*. We each need other people to help us see where we are still minimizing the harm that was done to us as children. For more on this, see chapter 13.

affair. After that conversation, my mom divorced my dad. But those were probably the only bad things that happened. No one ever hit me. I was never sexually abused. I certainly don't have any experiences of trauma or anything like that."

Do you see how this man is minimizing the heartache of his story? For an eleven-year-old boy to tell his mom that his dad is having an affair? Why didn't this man think of his experience as traumatic?

Because we all tend to minimize the harm we've experienced. It's natural and automatic.

For this man, having to tell his mom about his dad's affair was normal. That's just the way things were in his family. And so it felt normal and routine for him. Of course he didn't think it was harmful to his eleven-year-old self.

Anytime you compare your story to someone else's, you are minimizing your story. You are dressing the wounds of your childhood self as though they weren't serious. The sentence "My mom had a worse childhood than me" may be 100 percent true; however, you can use that sentence as a way to escape the heartache of *your* story.

Just because your story does not include a daring escape from a totalitarian regime in a war-torn country does not mean it is unworthy of engagement.

Here's the bottom line: you don't *want* your painful experiences to have affected you as much as they have, and so you don't give your stories the weight they deserve.

You don't want that jerk who hurt you so much as a child to still be affecting your life all these years later.

Anytime you compare your story to someone else's, you are escaping the heartache of your story. To be more precise: anytime you compare your story to someone else's story, you are engaged in self-contempt. *Self-contempt* is hatred or disdain for the younger you. Why do you feel disgust for that eleven-year-old boy? That fourteen-year-old girl? Why do you insist on dressing the wounds of that young person as though they were not serious? The presence of self-contempt always means you are minimizing the harm you endured as a child.

Another way you may be minimizing your story is by spiritualizing the bad things that have happened to you. *Spiritualizing* means using theology or the Bible to avoid feeling your big feelings, to avoid grappling with what actually happened to your heart, mind, and body when you were a child.

Have you ever used theology or the Bible to minimize the harm that was done to you?

If you have, you likely came by this practice honestly. The majority of evangelical churches are skilled at creating environments in which the harsh realities of living in a sinful world are spiritualized away. As Dan Allender has been saying for years, "The truth is largely lacking in our world."[3]

Suppose you've written a story about one of the times you were harmed as an eight-year-old. And you read the story to a friend. Your friend names how hard that experience must have been for an eight-year-old. As soon as your friend says this, you immediately respond with, "Yeah, it was hard, but I can see how God used that time to draw me closer to God and shape my character."

What are you doing in that moment? What's happening inside your brain and body? Most likely, you have begun to feel the discomfort of painful emotions, which is overwhelming. To lessen that overwhelm, you attempt to disconnect from the painful emotions by saying, "God used this bad experience for good."

If you use the name of God to downplay the pain of your past, you are using spirituality to avoid feeling your feelings. You're appealing

---

[3]. He's said this so many times, I have no idea when I first heard it. But they are his words.

to God's goodness to avoid sitting with that eight-year-old. To avoid drawing close to that child. You're evading the discomfort of your own story by saying, "Well, I know God works all things for good in my life and I can see how God was doing that even when I was being abused as an eight-year-old."

Please hear me well: I'm not disagreeing with the claim that God works all things for good in your life. I am wanting you to grapple with the question, Why do I need to bring up God or the Bible . . . *right now*? Right when your friend is giving weight to your pain and empathizing with you and offering to *be with you* in it?

We minimize our stories by spiritualizing away the ways we were harmed so that we don't have to feel our big feelings about how painful it all was.

WHAT IF I WASN'T ABUSED?

You may not believe your story was bad because you didn't experience overt abuse. You look back on your life and think, *I was never sexually abused and no one ever hit me, so I don't think I have a history of trauma/abuse*. My goal is not to convince you that you were abused. Some people escape childhood trauma and abuse. But no one escapes being harmed. Deeply. By their parents.

Moreover, the absence of overt abuse ("I was never hit or sexually molested") does not equate with "My story isn't that bad." What if you were never hit but were also never hugged? Never pursued or engaged with? What if you weren't sexually abused but were never touched at all?

If you grew up in a home that was devoid of deep relational connection, *how are you supposed to know that*? How are you supposed to know if you were *missing* something? Instead of feeling like "My parents were dismissive of me and unavailable," it is far more likely to have a sense of "My childhood was all right, I guess. Nothing really bad happened."

This is so important to understand. If you were missing something as a child, you likely didn't know it then, and it is often hard to see it even as an adult. Why aren't you going to know you were missing care, comfort, and connection? Because whatever level of care, comfort, and connection you received was *normal* for you. It's just the way things were for you as a child.

WHAT IF I DON'T REMEMBER MY STORY?

People often say to me, "I want to explore my story, but I don't remember anything from my growing-up years." My response is to ask, "Do you really not remember *anything*? Or do you remember some things . . . but you don't see how any of the things you do remember could possibly be affecting you today?"

I have never met someone who could not remember a single fragment of a story from their growing-up years. Most of us remember *something* from our past: a snippet of a memory from when you were seven, a short vignette from when you were in middle school.

It is likely that you do remember some stories (or partial stories) and are *minimizing* those stories by concluding they are "no big deal." In other words, you may say, "I don't remember anything," but what you really mean is "I don't remember anything significant or traumatic or harmful." You probably have partial stories you do remember, but you are dismissing them.

Let me say this as loudly as I can: ***don't be so sure that the stories you remember are no big deal.***

When I first began to reflect on my story, I remembered a couple of incidents that happened to me as a boy, but I thought to myself, *That wasn't a big deal. I don't see how that could still be affecting me today; it doesn't seem like a significant story. Who is going to want to hear about that?* However, now that other people have helped me better understand those very stories, I see they have had a profound effect on me and were very harmful. *But I didn't know that when I first wrote them down.* I felt foolish because they didn't seem significant or formative.

So, what if you wrote down one story you do remember, even if you don't see how that story could be affecting you today? *There is a reason you remember what you remember.*

Do you have a dismissive posture toward what you do remember? A dismissive posture means you have this sense of "I don't know why this story bothers me; it really was no big deal, but . . ." or "I don't know why I even remember this story, but I do." Why not write out that story and see what happens inside of you as you are writing it? See what emotions come up. See where the story takes you.

Next, get your hands on as many photo albums as you possibly can. Find every photo of yourself as a child, particularly photos in which you are not smiling. Retrieve every photo from birth to age eighteen, including your school portraits. Then carve out some quiet time to be alone and . . . just look at the photos.

[margin note: In the context of therapy?]

Notice what comes up inside as you are looking at the photos of yourself. Is there a particular photo that moves you? Makes you sad, makes you angry? If so, stop there and keep looking at it. Sit with the emotions that come up. Is there a particular photo you really don't like to look at for reasons you can't quite name? That matters. Your body is telling you something important. Be curious about why you don't like looking at it. See what memories come to mind as you are sitting with the picture.

If you struggle to remember details from a particular story, it is very common to feel hesitant to write out the story because you want to be truthful and honest.

I am glad you want to be truthful. But you need not be afraid of "making up a story."

Indeed, making up a story is not lying. Lying is far more about a refusal to tell the truth.

We tend to think "telling the truth" means recounting eyewitness testimony so that what we write accurately describes what a video recording of the incident would reveal. That's not what telling the truth is. In fact, we *can't* do that. The brain does not have the ability to perfectly recall the details of an incident.

Your brain does not have the capacity to write an eyewitness account that would perfectly match a video recording of the event. That's not how memory works. Don't let the fact that you don't remember everything perfectly keep you from writing the story.

In addition, you may have stories of experiences that happened so many times you don't remember any one particular incident. Since you can't remember any one particular incident, you don't feel like you can accurately write the story. For example, I have dozens of memories of my mom walking across the house to ask me for a hug. From a place of fragility, she would share something hard about her day as we hugged, and I knew it was my job to absorb some of her pain and use words to make her feel better about herself. This happened with such frequency that I don't remember any one time she did it. All the memories just blend together.

Please know this: you can write a truthful story that is an amalgamation of dozens or even hundreds of memories, even if you don't have explicit memory of one particular incident. When you make up a story that happened hundreds of times—even though you don't remember a particular episode—you are telling the truth.

CHAPTER 2 **KEY POINTS**

- There is a link between the ways your heart has been wounded and the ways you are hurting others, are stuck, or are bound. Your idolatry grows in the soil of your pain.
- You are likely dressing your wounds as though they are not serious.

- Anytime you say, "My story isn't that bad," you are minimizing your wounds by comparing your story to someone else's.
- Don't be so sure that the stories you remember are "no big deal."
- Your stories are worth exploring, even if you only remember fragments of scenes.
- Telling the truth about your past experiences does not require perfect recall.

3

COMMON OBJECTIONS TO EXPLORING YOUR STORY

It is very common to make a move toward exploring your story only to be quickly sidelined by internal objections to the entire endeavor. In this chapter, we'll address five common objections to exploring your story:

1. I should focus on the present and the future, not "dwell on the past."
2. Looking at my story is self-indulgent, introspective navel-gazing; I should be focused on God and others rather than focused on myself.
3. Who am I to judge or blame my parents? Jesus says, "Do not judge." Besides, I don't want to blame my parents.
4. There's no point in looking at how my parents hurt me because they did the best they could.
5. I can't change what's already happened, so what's the point of looking at the past?

Each of the above objections is reasonable. I had to personally work through each of them as I began engaging my story.

OBJECTION 1

I should focus on the present and the future, not "dwell on the past."

If you have been raised in the church, it is common to have a nagging sense that you are not supposed to dwell on the past. The idea is that if you spend too much time thinking about the past, you will somehow become stuck there. Weighed down. If you think about the past too much, it will do more harm than good. Indeed, the phrase "dwell on the past" has become pejorative in most Christian circles. Nobody uses the phrase in a positive way. Imagine recounting your day to a friend and saying, "I'm proud of myself. I spent an hour dwelling on my past."

But does God really want you to ignore your past story? I don't think so. One of the reasons I'm convinced God deeply values engaging your past is because the Bible devotes a great deal of space to doing just that. In other words, the Bible tells stories. Lots of stories. Seventy percent of the biblical text is narrative—devoted to telling stories about the past. Why would such a sizable portion of Scripture focus on recounting the past if God does not deeply value honoring what has been true about the past?

In Philippians 3, Paul says the following:

> Forgetting what is behind and straining toward what is ahead, I press on toward the goal to win the prize for which God has called me heavenward in Christ Jesus. (vv. 13–14)

If you take these verses out of context, Paul seems to be saying that Christians should forget the past and focus on the future. However, just a few verses earlier, Paul says this:

> I want to know Christ—yes, to know the power of his resurrection and participation in his sufferings, becoming like him in his death, and so, somehow, attaining to the resurrection from the dead. (vv. 10–11)

Paul's point is that you cannot experience resurrection (i.e., healing) until you know the fellowship of sharing in Christ's sufferings—until you know something of the death of Christ ("becoming like him in his death"). If you read all of Philippians 3, you'll see that Paul is not saying we should forget the past. On the contrary, he calls us to experientially know something of the suffering and death of Christ. But what does this mean?

You have experienced something of the suffering and death of Christ in your past story. You have known humiliation like Christ. You have been the object of another's contempt like Christ. You have experienced powerlessness like Christ.

What would it look like to follow Paul in wanting to know these sufferings more fully . . . so much so that you become like Christ in his death? What if knowing your sufferings more fully requires that you "dwell on the past" and engage your story?

OBJECTION 2

Looking at my story is self-indulgent, introspective navel-gazing; I should be focused on God and others rather than focused on myself.

This objection sounds so biblical! Self-centeredness is not a Christian virtue. Several years ago I heard a sermon in which the pastor said, "Some of you are way too focused on your story. Excessive introspection is simply another form of self-centeredness. Why not try thinking less about the bad things that have happened to you and thinking more about how you can love other people?" Again, this exhortation sounds biblical, but it's actually diabolical.

Why? One reason is because neuroscience research has shown that people who spend significant time reflecting on their past have an increased ability to empathize with others and care for others.[1] In

---

1. Daniel J. Siegel and Mary Hartzell, *Parenting from the Inside Out: How a Deeper Self-Understanding Can Help You Raise Children Who Thrive* (New York: Penguin, 2004), 123.

other words, exploring your past story increases your capacity to love others well.

Understanding your story is not an end in itself. Deep down, we all intuitively know that we are made for more than healing. Healing is beautiful . . . and there is more.

The ultimate purpose of engaging your story is to discover *who you are* and *what you are meant to do* during your time on earth. Said another way, the purpose of engaging your story is to discover *your kingdom*. In Luke 22, Jesus says to his disciples (and by extension to you and me), "I confer on you a kingdom" (v. 29).

You have a kingdom over which you rule.

Your kingdom includes all the people you impact by the unique ways you love. It includes all the ways you bring beauty into your corner of the world.

Your kingdom is different from mine . . . and this is true not because we have different gifts but because we have different stories. In other words, if you want to identify the particularities of the kingdom Jesus has conferred on you, then you have to understand your past story.

This is because the harm you have experienced is not random. Evil has assaulted you precisely in the areas in which you most reflect the beauty and glory of God. For example, if you were exquisitely sensitive as a young child, it is likely your sensitivity has been cursed and shamed. If you were particularly imaginative and open to a sense of wonder, it is likely these attributes in particular have been assaulted.

Identify how you have been harmed, and you will be a step closer to knowing something specific about your kingdom.

The story of Joseph culminates with Genesis 50:20, where Joseph says, "You intended to harm me, but God intended it for good." This sentence is intended to be a banner over each person's story, including yours.

To look at your story is to identify how God took the wounds inflicted by evil and used those very wounds to equip you to rule over your kingdom.

Here's the point: reflecting on your stories of harm and heartache is precisely what is required to know something about what you are called to do in this world.

OBJECTION 3

Who am I to judge or blame my parents? Jesus says, "Do not judge." Besides, I don't want to blame my parents.

It is impossible to explore your story without making judgments about other people in your story, including your parents. Many Christians begin engaging their story, but their good endeavor comes to a screeching halt with the objection, "It's not my place to judge my parents. I shouldn't be doing this."

The reasoning is simple: "Jesus says not to judge people. So who am I to judge my parents' actions toward me? I don't know their full story. I don't know why they did what they did to me. It's God's job to judge my parents, not mine."

Again, this objection sounds biblical at first glance, but it's not. When most people say, "I'm not supposed to judge my parents," they appeal to Jesus's teaching from Matthew 7, which begins, "Do not judge, or you too will be judged." But a close reading of Matthew 7 shows that Jesus is actually *calling* us to judge our parents (and everyone else we want to love well).[2]

---

2. A massive amount of harm has been done by people who identify as Christian and have no problem passing judgment on others and condemning them. There are scores of self-righteous evangelicals who judge others in a way that excludes them from full participation in the body of Christ. When I am speaking about judging others, I do not mean condemning anyone from a position of self-righteousness. I mean accurately naming someone from a position of wanting to honor them enough to name what is true.

> Do not judge, or you too will be judged. For in the same way you judge others, you will be judged, and with the measure you use, it will be measured to you.
>
> Why do you look at the speck of sawdust in your brother's eye and pay no attention to the plank in your own eye? How can you say to your brother, "Let me take the speck out of your eye," when all the time there is a plank in your own eye? You hypocrite, first take the plank out of your own eye, and then you will see clearly to remove the speck from your brother's eye. (vv. 1–5)

What is the trajectory of this teaching that begins with "Do not judge"? What is Jesus's point? Jesus's point is that he wants us to become the kind of men and women who see clearly enough to remove the speck from another person's eye. In other words, the whole point of this teaching that begins with "Do not judge" is that you and I are called to judge other people—and to judge them well.

Think about it. How can you remove the speck from another person's eye if you have not first judged that person *as having a speck in their eye*? A speck is a metaphor for something in the other person's heart that is sinful or harmful. How can you remove the sinful speck if you have not first named and identified it?

As you explore your story, you will inevitably find moments when your parents harmed you (because your parents are sinners just like you). According to Matthew 7, your task is to help remove the specks from their eyes. You can't remove the speck from your dad's eye until you have first identified the speck (named your dad's sin). The whole point of Jesus's teaching here is that we are to be the kind of people who love others actively enough that we are willing to reach into their eyes—getting right up in their personal space—and gently remove the speck from their eyes.

In the conclusion of this teaching, Jesus says, "Do not give dogs what is sacred; do not throw your pearls to pigs" (v. 6). What is the sacred pearl Jesus is referring to? It is precisely your willingness to name the other person's speck—your willingness to gently point out the other person's sin. When you take the risk of saying, "Mom, this is what it was like having you as a mother," you are giving your mom a pearl. This is part of how we love one another well.

So, if Jesus calls us to judge, why does he begin with "Do not judge"?

When Jesus says, "Do not judge," he is using the word *judge* to refer to a posture of *condemning* the other person. The word translated "judge" is based on the Greek word *krinō*. This root word is also used in Romans 8:1, where Paul writes, "There is now no condemnation for those who are in Christ Jesus." The word translated "condemnation" is *katakrino*—*kata* meaning against and *krinō* meaning judgment. *Katakrino* is judgment *against*—condemnation. Jesus is warning us against *condemning* our parents, not judging them. Condemning another person is very different from naming their sin and identifying their speck. Jesus is not warning you against judgment per se, but judgment *against*. A spirit of condemnation is very different from a posture of "I love you enough that I am willing to name your sin and help you remove it."

It is very common to begin taking a peek at some of the ways your parents wounded you only to be met with an internal feeling of *I don't want to be one of those people who blames my parents for everything*.

First of all, I am not inviting you to blame your parents for everything. Your parents are not responsible for all of your wounds. Second, there is a difference between blaming and *naming*. Blame is about having a posture of contempt toward another person. Blame is a pointed finger that seeks to expose someone so you can condemn them. There is a difference between blaming your father and naming what has been true about your relationship with him. There is a difference between wanting to condemn your mother and wanting to have a candid conversation with her about how she harmed you.

I have two adolescent children. In five or ten years, they are going to sit me down and say, "Dad, here's what it was like to have you as a father. Here's what it was like to be parented by an ambivalently attached man who was often dysregulated. Let me tell you what that was like for me. Let me tell you some of the ways you wounded me."

When my children say this to me, it will be one of the holiest moments of my life. *They're not blaming me.* They're giving me the opportunity to participate in their healing by owning how I harmed them and seeking to repair the damage I've done.

I want my children to feel the freedom to tell me how I wounded them.

OBJECTION 4

There's no point in looking at how my parents hurt me because they did the best they could.

Hundreds of people have sat in my office and said, "I'll admit that my parents harmed me, but they did the best they could." This is a very odd objection for Christians to hold. Why? Because according to the Bible, *no one does the best they can all the time.*

Everyone's a sinner. Sometimes we do our best and sometimes we don't do our best. But no one tries their best all the time.

As a high school and college student, I loved the Sermon on the Mount. It was one of those passages that I was particularly fond of . . . until Dan Allender ruined it for me. How do you ruin the Sermon on the Mount?

Dan pointed out that in Matthew 5 Jesus talks about lust and anger. Dan went on to say that Jesus's point is that everyone is an adulterer (everyone lusts) and everyone is a murderer (everyone rages). And then Dan had the audacity to suggest that "everyone" included my parents.

I knew I had adulterous lust and murderous rage inside of me, but I wasn't sure my parents did. Yet this is precisely what Jesus is saying.³ Indeed, the claim of the Bible is that all people—even your parents—are sinful. This means there were times when your father didn't do the best he could. There were moments when your mother didn't do her best either.

We hide behind "my parents did their best" because we don't want to look at the reality of the sin in their hearts and how deeply they hurt us. If everyone is a sinner, have you named the ways your mother sinned against you? Your father?

OBJECTION 5

I can't change what's already happened, so what's the point of looking at the past?

In his novel *Requiem for a Nun*, William Faulkner writes, "The past is never dead. It's not even past."⁴ If you think your past is in the past, you don't understand how the brain functions. Whenever you have an experience in the present, the first thing your brain does is filter that experience through all your past experiences.

In other words, *no one experiences the reality of the present moment as it truly is*. That notion is a fiction based on a misunderstanding of how the brain comes to be formed and how it operates. You experience reality through the lens of what you have already experienced. You see more of what you've already seen.

Why? Because God designed your brain to have neurons, and that's how neurons work. As mentioned earlier, neurons are connected with one another. As the classic neuroscience saying goes, "Neurons that fire together, wire together."⁵ Neurons that are closely

---

3. When Jesus uses the word *lust* in Matthew 5:28, he is talking about much more than sexual lust. The Greek word translated here, *epithymeō*, implies *all* desires that have become immediate demands: "I want what I want and I must have it now."
4. William Faulkner, *Requiem for a Nun* (New York: Vintage Books, 1975), 80.
5. Neuropsychologist Donald Hebb introduced this concept in 1949 to describe how pathways in the brain are formed and reinforced through repetition. See Carla Shatz,

connected to each other (wired together) tend to fire together again and again and again.

When I was a boy, my mother looked to me for emotional connection, comfort, and companionship. My father was emotionally checked out due to his PTSD. He was not attuned to my mother. My mother's response to this heartache was to train me to be attuned to her. In time, I knew I was required to be very attentive to Mom's needs, and to meet those needs as best I could.

I became hyperattuned to my mom's emotional states. I knew when she needed me to tend to her, to talk with her about what was troubling her . . . things my father should have been doing.

In short, my brain learned that when my mother was upset, it was my job to make her feel better.

Now—here's the point—decades later, when a woman is upset, I feel like it's my job to tend to her and comfort her and make her world okay again. Why? Because I have neurons . . . and that's how neurons operate.

In other words, the neurons that tell me "a woman is upset" are connected to neurons that say, "Adam, spring into action and comfort that woman."

The reason that the past isn't dead, the reason that it's not even past, is because of this thing called *priming*. My brain has been primed to think that when a woman is upset, it's my job to make her feel better.

So, let me turn this objection of "I can't change what's already happened, so what's the point?" on its head: the point of exploring your past story is so that *you can actually live in the present.* Until you engage your past story, you are actually living as much in the past as you are in the present. That is, your brain is filtering your present experiences through the unmetabolized wounds

---

"The Developing Brain," *Scientific American* 267 (1992): 60–67.

from your growing-up years. That's how neural networks work. As you become clear about your wounds and address them, the filters begin to fade, and you are able to live increasingly in the present.

Dan Allender is fond of provocatively saying, "Few things are easier to change than your past." His point is that the way you have made sense of your past story is likely wrong. Why? Because there are many family truths that a child's brain cannot bear.

For example, a seven-year-old brain cannot let in the reality that your father prefers your older sister to you. A ten-year-old brain cannot let in the reality that your mother prefers your older brother to you. A thirteen-year-old brain cannot let in the reality that your stepfather is molesting you on a regular basis. In short, a child or adolescent brain cannot let in the reality of harm from the two people who are supposed to protect you and delight in you. As a result, your brain's only option is to form a deeply flawed narrative. My flawed narrative was this: "God gave me a kind and loving mother to compensate for a physically and emotionally abusive father."

How do you change your past? By becoming clear about the truth of your story. The narrative reveals the truth that was always there but could not be seen by a child's eyes.

It took me several years to rewrite my narrative to "My mother trained me to be her surrogate spouse, which set me up to be envied and hated by my father."

When you accurately name the truth of your story, your brain changes. As your brain changes, you begin to see the present more clearly.

The claim of the gospel is that you can absolutely change the past. You can't change the events; you can't make the wounds not happen. But you can receive healing—which means your brain can change. The way your brain remembers the event can absolutely change. When God heals, your brain changes. Your neurons become rewired.

What "attaining to the resurrection from the dead" (Phil. 3:11) means in neurobiological terms is the rewiring of the cells that make up your brain. In other words, Dan Allender is right: few things are easier to change than your past.

CHAPTER 3 **KEY POINTS**

- Many people believe that dwelling on the past hinders spiritual progress; however, the Bible values storytelling and understanding your past.
- Although reflecting on your story is often viewed as self-indulgent, neuroscience demonstrates that reflecting on the past enhances empathy and increases your ability to love others well.
- Jesus calls each of us to honest evaluation of others (including our parents); condemnation is different than judgment.
- Acknowledging the failures of your parents is crucial for healing and growth.
- The past influences present perceptions and behaviors through the process of neural priming; engaging your past allows you to increasingly live in the present.

4

WHAT IF YOU ENGAGED YOUR FAMILY OF ORIGIN STORY?

> Far more crucial than what we know or do not know is what we do not want to know.
>
> Eric Hoffer, *The Passionate State of Mind*

When it comes to engaging your story, there's a sense in which the most significant plotline of that story is your relationship with your parents.[1] It's certainly the most influential in terms of setting the trajectory for your life.

Why is this the case? My reading of the neuroscience literature has led me to formulate what I call the first and second laws of neurobiological development:

> Law #1: Relationships influence the brain more than anything else. More than drugs, more than nutrition, more than exercise, more than meditation, more than anything.[2]

---

1. Throughout this book I will use the term *parent* in a broad sense. Many people grew up in nontraditional families in which the family structure was different from "Mom and Dad." Some were raised by single parents, stepparents, grandparents, adopted parents—there are many family structures. When I use the term *parents*, I am referring to your primary caregivers, whoever that may have been.
2. Siegel and Hartzell, *Parenting from the Inside Out*, 101–2.

Law #2: Your earliest life experiences have a much more significant influence on your brain than your later life experiences.[3]

When we put these two laws together, we get the following implication: our earliest relationship with our primary caretakers has had the most shaping power on our brains.

Remember, each of us is created in the image of a triune God—a "we" and not an "I." You are created in the image of a "we." Perhaps a more helpful name for the Trinity is "The Relationship." You are created in the image of The Relationship. What does this mean, practically? It means you are built for connection with others. It's hardwired into your very being. Your brain and body are intended to be in deep connection with other brains and bodies. Which brings us to the very important topic of attachment.

ATTACHMENT

Attachment refers to the manner in which you connect with others. It's the emotional bond you develop with the people you are closest to. The people who are there for you, and who truly know you.

If your primary caregivers were sufficiently attuned, responsive, and engaged with you as a child, you developed what is called a *secure attachment*, which is a really big deal. A securely attached adult has:

> The ability to regulate his or her affect (more on this later).
>
> Built-in resilience to stress.
>
> The ability to make sense of his or her story and life experiences in a coherent way, which is very important for brain health.

---

3. Allan N. Schore, *The Science of the Art of Psychotherapy*, Norton Series on Interpersonal Neurobiology (New York: W. W. Norton, 2012), 52–70. The brain grows at a very rapid rate for the first couple years of your life, and then it slows down.

> A high likelihood of being in relationship with other securely attached people and having healthy, fulfilling, and meaningful relationships.[4]

If I am securely attached as a child, I will have an embodied sense of knowing that I *matter* to my primary caregivers, they *want* to be in relationship with me, and they will *respond* to my needs.

When securely attached children become adults, they live in a continual state of relational hopefulness. Securely attached adults anticipate that when there is relational rupture—when there is interpersonal conflict—the relationship will be restored. It's only a matter of time, and it will come about without either person having to stuff their feelings or sacrifice their individuality—that is, their perspective on the conflict.

The essence of secure attachment in adulthood is the ability to both self-regulate *and* reach for help—that is, you can look to others to interactively regulate you and have confidence that they will be available to soothe you. Secure attachment does not mean you are always able to self-regulate. It means you can self-regulate at times and, at other times, vulnerably reach for help from another when you need it.

Now, how are you supposed to know if you are securely attached? One way is to look at the story of your relationship with your parents. Children need six things from their primary caregivers in order to develop a secure attachment. I call these "the Big Six" because they are *oh so very important*. The presence or absence of these six things sets the trajectory for the rest of your relational life. If you received them from your parents, you will be a securely attached adult. If you did not, you will be insecurely attached.[5]

---

4. Siegel and Hartzell, *Parenting from the Inside Out*, 102–3.
5. It's important to understand that your relationship with one parent was different from your relationship with the other. As a result, you can be securely attached to one parent but insecurely attached to the other. In addition, your attachment style can change as you heal and mature. Insecure attachment is changeable; it is not fixed. As you engage your story and begin to heal, you will increasingly become a more securely attached adult.

THE BIG SIX

1. Attunement

The first thing every child needs from their parents to form a secure attachment is attunement, which refers to your parents' desire and ability to read your emotional state.

Were your parents paying sufficient attention to you that they knew something of what you were feeling on the inside? A parent who is distracted and preoccupied by their own needs, emotions, or personal pain cannot be attuned to their child's needs.

When you are on the receiving end of attunement, you "feel felt."[6] You have a sense that the other person really gets what is happening inside of you. *You know they know* what you are feeling. As a result, you feel joined by them.

This is the first thing you needed from your parents. You needed to feel felt. You needed to feel like your mother got you. And that she wanted to get you, wanted to understand you.

> When I was about six years old, we lived in Fairport, New York. Not many people had outdoor pools, but my dad told me that one of his coworkers did have one. That summer, I was very excited about the prospect of swimming in that pool. One hot Saturday in August, I was bored all day long. Toward the end of the day I complained to my dad about how bored I had been. My dad responded by saying, "I wish I had known that earlier because my coworker invited us over to the pool today, but I told him that I didn't think you would want to go." I was devastated. Crushed. I can still remember the feeling to this day.
>
> The most devastating part of this experience to me was not the fact that I didn't get to swim in the pool; the most devastating part was the sinking feeling I had in my stomach when I realized that

---

[6]. Siegel and Hartzell, *Parenting from the Inside Out*, 108.

my dad didn't know how badly I wanted to swim in that pool and how much I had been looking forward to it all summer.

As you think back on your growing-up years, did you feel felt by your parents? Were you attuned to? When you were in second grade, did you have a sense that your mom wanted to know what was happening inside of you? When you were a sophomore in high school, did you have a sense that your dad cared about what was going on for you emotionally?[7]

If your parents were not frequently attuned to you, your heart has been wounded—because God created children with a deep need for attunement.

2. Responsiveness

The second thing every child needs from their parents is responsiveness. If attunement refers to reading your face at the dinner table, responsiveness refers to what your parents *did* with the sad face they saw at the dinner table. Did your mother respond to you when you were distressed?

When you were mad, sad, or afraid, did your father read that you were feeling those things, and did he respond to you in a meaningful way? Did he offer comfort, care, and kindness?

Your dad knew you were upset after your soccer game. Did he sit on the edge of your bed that night and ask you about your disappointment?

---

7. Most of us have the sense that one of our parents was more attuned to us than the other. This is natural; however, here's a word of caution: suppose your father was physically present but emotionally absent—suppose he was rarely attuned to you. As an adult, you may *feel* like your mom was attuned to you because, after all, she was way more attuned to you than your father. However, this does not necessarily mean your mother was attuned to you. It simply means that relative to your father, you felt more attunement from your mother. When a child is starving, crumbs can feel like a substantial meal. This relativity will be true throughout the Big Six. You have a unique relationship with each parent.

When you had a hard day at school, what was it like for you to come home and see your mother? You have to understand that your parents saw your face when you had a terrible day in middle school. *They saw your face.* Did they respond to what they saw?

When something bad happened to you—like sexual abuse from a neighbor, perhaps—and you told your mom about it, did she respond to you? You may be thinking, *I never would have told my mother if something like that happened.* Have you ever thought about why? If you never would have told your mom, it is likely because you learned from a very young age that *it wouldn't matter* if you told Mom. You knew she was not going to respond to you in a way that brought comfort and care to your heart.

Every child needs their parents to be responsive to them when they are feeling big feelings like anger, sadness, or fear.

> When I was in seventh grade, I didn't have much hair on my legs. A rumor started that I shaved my legs. Two kids were the ringleaders, but eventually a dozen of my peers joined in. When they saw me in the halls, they would either make razor noises at me or look at me and yell, "Shave your legs!" All the other kids could hear it. All the other kids knew I wasn't doing anything about it.
>
> I lived in a state of fear and hypervigilance. I felt completely powerless—I never knew when it would happen, who would do it, who would be around to hear it, or how long it would last. I hated myself for not fighting them, for not sticking up for myself, for not stopping the teasing. But I froze every time it happened. I felt paralyzed.
>
> I was an anxious wreck day in and day out, especially before school. And my parents knew this. They saw my face each day. Here's the point: as a seventh grader, I desperately needed my parents to respond to what they knew was going on, to respond to the humiliation and fear I felt every morning. I needed them to talk with me and help me decide how I wanted to handle this situation. But they didn't.

In contrast to the above, one of my best memories with my father happened during an incredibly painful season of my life.

I was twenty years old and had taken a semester off from college. I was experiencing debilitating anxiety and depression. One day I was crying in my parents' bedroom. Sitting next to my dad on a gray couch, I said through tears, "Dad, I just didn't know life could be this painful." My dad's face broke, and he began to cry too. He reached out and hugged me. It was one of the sweetest moments I ever shared with my father. He responded to me and my pain with his whole being. I'll never forget it.

A word of caution for parents: if you have children, you are going to be tempted to begin thinking about whether or not you are providing these six things for your children rather than thinking about whether or not you *received* these six things as a child. I understand your desire to parent your children well; however, this tendency to focus on our parenting failures rather than focusing on the ways we were failed by our parents allows us to avoid feeling the pain of our own story.

Moreover, the single greatest gift you can give your children is to think deeply about what it was like *for you* as a child—in other words, to make sense of your own developmental story. Research has demonstrated that if you want to improve your parenting, the number-one thing you can do is to engage your family of origin story and make sense of your life experiences.[8]

Neuroscientist Dan Siegel puts it like this: "The best predictor of how our children will become attached to us is how well we have come to make sense of our lives, how well we tell a coherent story of our early life experiences."[9]

So, please, as you read about the Big Six, resist the urge to think about your parenting and instead think about your experience as a child.

---

8. Siegel and Hartzell, *Parenting from the Inside Out*, 123.
9. Siegel and Hartzell, *Parenting from the Inside Out*, 123.

3. Engagement

The third thing every child needs from their parents is engagement. Engagement means your mom and dad wanted to know you—the real you, with all of your quirks—and they sought to draw you out. *Engagement* means your parents had a genuine desire to know your inner emotional world, and they pursued you.

Did your father have an internal intention and genuine desire to truly know your heart? Was he willing to engage with you on a deep level? Did you feel pursued by your mother?

It's not enough for a child to be attuned to and responded to. There has to be a pursuit of the child's heart. A drawing out of their hopes, dreams, fears, and desires.

Neuroscientist Curt Thompson is fond of saying that when each one of us comes into this world, we enter it looking for someone looking for us. Our deepest desire is that there will be someone looking for us, and that this person will always be there for us and will pursue our hearts with a genuine desire to truly know us.

> If my dad wasn't working, he was probably "outside with his plants." That's the phrase Mom and I used whenever one of us asked the other, "Where's Dad?" Throughout middle and high school, I was desperate for my father's presence. I had a deep longing to know him, and an equally deep longing for my father to know me. And so I would often go out in the yard where all the plants were . . . looking for my father.
>
> If my dad was planting a new plant, I would simply stand there next to him. Getting as close to him as he'd allow, I'd make multiple bids for connection. I might ask him about his work or tell him about something happening at school or—when I was really brave—ask him about Vietnam.
>
> These were all desperate attempts to hear my father's voice. I didn't know it at the time, but I was working very hard to create

the right environment for my dad to open up to me. And for my dad to pursue me and ask me about me. I was trying to make it as easy as possible for him to father me. But it never worked.

Each of us is born with a question deep inside: Does my father/mother delight in me?

We need to know in the center of our hearts that the two people who brought us into the world delight in us. It's the sense of, "You are a beloved child. I enjoy being with you. I like who you are." If the deepest part of your heart never got the message that your parents delighted in you—or if one did and the other didn't—you carry a wound inside your heart.

Did your heart remain undiscovered by your parents? If it did, that had a big impact on your brain and your attachment style.

4. Ability to Regulate Your Affect

Affect refers to the felt sense of what is happening in your physical body. Affect is your moment-to-moment experience of your internal bodily sensations. Think of affect on a scale of 1–10, where 1 represents numb and shut down and 10 represents panic or rage. On this scale, 5–6 represents a slight feeling of relaxed excitement—alert, present, and attentive. Hopefully, you are in the 5–6 range right now.

When you are in the 5–6 range, you are regulated. It's the zone of optimal arousal.[10] When you dip down into the 1–3 range, you enter a dysregulated state known as *hypoarousal*. Hypoarousal is marked by bodily sensations such as a sense of numbness or feeling shut down, shallow breathing, and difficulty concentrating. When you are hypoaroused, you are often feeling some combination of shame, hopelessness, and/or despair.

When you amp up to the 8–10 range, you enter a dysregulated state known as *hyperarousal*. Hyperarousal is marked by bodily sensations

---

10. Here, *arousal* is a synonym for affect; it does not refer to sexual arousal.

such as a racing heart, faster breathing, a tightening in the chest or stomach, or a sense of jitteriness. When you are hyperaroused, you are often feeling some combination of panic, terror, and/or rage.

So, affect exists on a continuum. It ranges from numb and shut down (1–3), through relaxed and attentive (5–6), and on to panicked and frenzied (8–10).

As an infant and young child, you became dysregulated *all the time*. Many, many times a day. Infants have absolutely no ability to regulate their own affect. You couldn't calm your body when it got anxious or stimulate your body when it became shut down and listless. Infants are completely dependent on their parents to regulate their affect for them.[11]

But what if your mother was so preoccupied by her own trauma—or her own big feelings—that she couldn't soothe you and regulate you? Or what if your father was emotionally checked out and didn't want to soothe you when you were dysregulated?

In that case, it was very difficult for you to develop the brain structures necessary for self-regulation. Why? Because the way a child's brain develops the neurobiological structures to self-regulate is by having their affect interactively regulated by parents who are attuned, responsive, and engaged. When the primary caregivers are unable or unwilling to regulate the child, the child's brain fails to develop the necessary neural networks for self-regulation.

> Amelia came to see me because, in her words, she had "lost control of her emotions" ever since her second baby arrived. As we explored her story growing up, Amelia told me about failing to make the gymnastics team her junior year in high school. She was a very good gymnast, especially on beam and bars. However, on the last day of tryouts, she made a few small mistakes on beam. As she put it, "None of these mistakes would have kept me off the team,

---

11. Schore, *Science of the Art of Psychotherapy*, 229.

but I started to panic inside and the panic resulted in big mistakes . . . and the big mistakes were the end of my gymnastics career." Although she didn't use this language, Amelia clearly became very dysregulated during that final day of tryouts. Dysregulation does not make for a good beam routine. From the middle of her beam routine all the way until the end of tryouts, Amelia was furious at herself for not being able to calm her body. She felt deep shame about falling apart like that. As she recounted the story, she also told me about meeting her mom in the parking lot at the end of the day. Amelia burst into tears as soon as she got in the car. Completely dysregulated, she began yelling and screaming about how she was her own worst enemy.

In this moment, Amelia desperately needed her mother to be a mother and provide containment and care. When you are dysregulated and feeling very big feelings, your brain needs a psychological "container" for those feelings. This container is the regulated presence of another person who is *there for you,* so that you can feel and express your big feelings. In this way, children learn how to express their emotions and manage their dysregulated bodies.

However, Amelia's role in her family was *to regulate her mother* when Mom was overwhelmed or anxious. In many ways, their roles were reversed. Amelia provided significantly more affect regulation for her mother than vice versa. In the car that day, Amelia's mother became just as dysregulated as Amelia about the situation. As a result, Amelia was left utterly alone in her dysregulation with no one to help her manage it.

What about for you? Think back to elementary school—did your mother help regulate you when you were distressed (afraid, mad, sad, ashamed)? Think back to middle school—when you were anxious, did your father see your anxiety and help calm you down and bring regulation to your body? Or were you left alone when you were in need of regulation and soothing and care?

5. Ability to Handle Your Big Emotions

As a child, you needed your parents to have the emotional strength to bring some containment to your so-called negative emotions (anger, fear, sadness). You needed the freedom to express those emotions—to cry, rage, or fall silent—knowing you would be responded to in a loving, meaningful way. You needed to know deep down that your big emotions were accepted and allowed in the home.

Did your parents welcome your anger, sadness, and fear? Were you allowed to be sad and to cry as a kid? Were you allowed to be angry? Or did your parents communicate (verbally or nonverbally) that big emotions were somehow "bad" and off-limits?

You needed to feel the freedom to say to your mother, "I hate you" or "You don't love me," knowing you would not be met with "Go to your room!" or "How could you say that?" or "Don't you know that hurts Mommy's feelings?"

Could you yell at your mother without her getting a look on her face of "How could you say that?" Could you yell at your father without him raging at you or giving you the silent treatment? You needed to know deep down that your emotions were accepted and allowed—even welcomed. As Brent Curtis so beautifully puts it, perhaps your family was "too fragile to bear the weight of [your] unedited soul."[12]

Imagine you're a twelve-year-old girl who is trying to survive middle school. After a particularly hard day, you are alone in your room and your mom comes in. You tell Mom a little bit about what happened between you and some other girls who were cruel. Through tears, you explain why you are so upset. Instead of being strong enough to handle your big emotions, your mom looks at you and says, "Honey, maybe you're just too sensitive."

---

12. Brent Curtis, "Less-Wild Lovers: Standing at the Crossroads of Desire," *Mars Hill Review* 8 (Summer 1997): 9–23.

In that moment, your twelve-year-old heart is deeply wounded. When you most need empathy, you are met with reproach. The message is clear: *Your feelings are out of proportion, and maybe the problem is with you.* You don't just recover from that with time.

> Rachel, a sophomore in college, came to see me because she was experiencing overwhelming anxiety. She was terrified that she couldn't make her anxiety decrease. One afternoon she crawled into bed and pulled the covers over her head.
>
> Eventually, Rachel's father came in to check on her. He didn't say anything; he simply paced around the room and eventually sat down on Rachel's bed. He knew she was filled with anxiety and terrified. In time, father and daughter began to talk a little. Rachel's dad asked her if she knew what she was so anxious about. She replied by saying, "I'm not sure, but my counselor thinks my anxiety is caused by years of stuffed anger at you."
>
> Rachel's dad's face immediately changed to an expression of fury. He stood up, and with a rage-filled voice started yelling at her. "Look, if anyone in this house deserves to be angry, it's me. Everyone in this house has been blaming me for causing all this anxiety in you. You know, Rachel, maybe I should just leave." And then he walked out of Rachel's room, leaving her alone.

What happened? Rachel took the risk of expressing a very small portion of her big feelings, and her dad couldn't handle it. His shame immediately turned into contempt for Rachel. Instead of feeling seen and comforted by her dad, she felt guilty for making him want to leave the family. Plus, Rachel felt terror that he might actually leave.

Remembering how neurons operate (what fires together, wires together), consider what happens in a young brain on days like the one Rachel experienced. We learn that if we tell someone about our pain, we will end up feeling even more alone, plus we will feel shame and self-contempt for hurting the other person. It's better to stay alone in our pain and not say anything. This is the kind of thing that happens when a parent isn't strong enough to handle a child's big emotions.

6. Willingness to Repair Rupture

Finally, as a child you needed your parents to be willing to repair harm when they wounded you. It's hard to overstate the importance of repair when it comes to the healthy development of a child's brain. Brains develop best in an environment of trust and safety. Trust and safety are not primarily a function of perfect attunement, perfect responsiveness, and so forth. Indeed, trust and safety are not built on the absence of failure but on the willingness of the parent to own and rectify failures when they do occur.

No parent gets attunement right 100 percent of the time. No parent is always responsive and engaged. The parent-child connection ruptures frequently. This is no big deal! What mattered to you as a child was not that your parents got it right every time but that they recognized when they hurt you and responded in a way that brought comfort and reconnection. In other words, what mattered was that your parents recognized relational rupture and then reconnected with you by repairing that rupture.

If a parent is unwilling to own their failure and unwilling to repair the harm they have done, the child will often feel crazy. This is because the child knows they didn't deserve such a severe beating and, at the same time, can't make sense of the situation any other way. The child simultaneously knows it isn't their fault and that it must be their fault, and so a war rages inside them.

One way the child often deals with this feeling of craziness is to dismiss what their heart and body know about their innocence and conclude they must be bad. Suppose a mother loses her temper with her son, screams at him, and hits him. If the mother doesn't come back later that night and acknowledge her wrongdoing, the child will either feel crazy or conclude that there is something wrong with him. Children are meaning-making creatures. A child's brain needs a coherent narrative to make sense of the world. Absent an apology from his mother, the only way for the boy to make the narrative coherent is to conclude, *There must be something wrong with me.*

So, think back on your childhood. When your parents hurt you, did they own their failure? Do you remember your mother coming to you and saying, "Honey, I'm sorry I lost my temper. I was wrong to do that, and I'm sorry"? How many times did your father sit you down and say, "It was wrong for me to say what I said, and I'm sorry"? When was the last time you heard your father say a heartfelt, "I was wrong to do such and such"?

> I was twenty-six years old before I risked saying *ouch* to my mother. *Twenty-six years old.* If you think back on your growing-up years and can't remember a time when you told your parents how hurt you were by something they said or did, then *there is a reason for that.*
>
> You learned at a very young age that telling your parents about your hurt, sorrow, or anger at them would not go well.
>
> When I was twenty-six, I had just graduated from my social work program, and my parents told me they would not be able to come to my graduation ceremony. It happened that my graduation ceremony was the same weekend as my sister-in-law's college graduation, so immediately after my ceremony was done on Friday night, my wife and I flew from Virginia to Ohio to attend her graduation on Saturday. As I saw all her family members celebrating her, deep sorrow and disappointment kicked in.
>
> After the ceremony, we went to a graduation party for my sister-in-law, and I was so upset that my parents had not come to my graduation that I decided to call my mother and tell her.
>
> I couldn't hold it in anymore. I went to an empty bedroom in the house and called home. My mom answered the phone.

"Mom," I said, "I'm at Caroline's sister's graduation, and I'm realizing how disappointed and upset I am that you and Dad didn't come to my graduation yesterday." I risked expressing disappointment in my mother.

My mother became frantic and started crying. Everything changed in an instant. Through panicky tears she said, "Adam, this is really hard for your father and me. You choose to spend all this time with Caroline's family and none with us. You visit them. You go on vacation with them. You seem to like them more." I could hear Mom's sobs and feel her franticness through the telephone line.

And a very familiar shift happened inside of me. In my core, I moved from "feeling and expressing my disappointment" to "feeling sadness for my mother's pain." Without thinking about what I was doing, I took the phone and went into the closet and closed the door. It was pitch black in there.

I was getting alone with my mother.

I was so scared in that closet—scared of losing my mom. As a twenty-six-year-old. And, at the same time, I felt immense sadness and guilt because I was causing Mom pain. I instantly pushed down my own feelings of deep disappointment to tend to my mother's sadness and franticness. After reassuring and comforting my mother, I hung up the phone.

Sitting alone in that dark closet—stunned, confused, and feeling spun around—I thought to myself, *What just happened? I called home to tell Mom I was hurt, and it turned into a conversation about how I was hurting her.*

This type of experience is very common when one of your parents is unwilling to repair harm or even bear the fact that he or she has harmed you.

It's important to understand that no parent can possibly be 100 percent attuned, responsive, and engaged. So, how much is enough for a child to develop a healthy brain? Attachment expert Ed Tronick points out that parents of securely attached children demonstrate attunement and responsiveness on the first try about 33 percent of the time! Only one time in three! The reason these children are securely attached is the parents notice when they are mis-attuning to their children and offer repair most of the time.[13]

CHAPTER 4 KEY POINTS

- To make sense of your story, you have to understand your relationship with your parents when you were growing up.
- Your earliest relationship with your primary caretakers has significantly shaped the development of your brain.
- The way you attached to your primary caregivers profoundly influences how you presently relate to other people.
- Secure attachment occurs when you receive the following six things as a child: attunement, responsiveness, engagement, affect regulation, strength to handle your big emotions, and willingness to repair rupture.

---

13. Edward Z. Tronick, "'Of Course All Relationships Are Unique': How Co-Creative Processes Generate Unique Mother-Infant and Patient-Therapist Relationships and Change Other Relationships," *Psychoanalytic Inquiry* 23, no. 3 (2003): 473–91.

THE BIG SIX EXERCISE

Carve out some unhurried time to complete the following exercise. This is a critical part of exploring your story. You cannot understand your story—you cannot understand how your brain has been shaped—without understanding the degree to which these six things were met for you in childhood.

Instructions. Think back to your growing-up years, ages 4–18. Rate the items below on a scale of 1 to 5.

1=Never, 2=Rarely, 3=Occasionally, 4=Sometimes, 5=Often

1. **Attunement** refers to your parents' ability to read you, to seek to know what you are feeling and experiencing on the inside.

   _____ My mother was attuned to my emotional state. She knew when I was feeling big emotions like anger, sadness, or fear. When I was upset about something, she knew it. She was able to read my face and my tone of voice. She knew when I needed or wanted something.

   _____ My father was attuned to my emotional state. He knew when I was feeling big emotions like anger, sadness, or fear. When I was upset about something, he knew it. He was able to read my face and my tone of voice. He knew when I needed or wanted something.

How consistent was your parents' level of attunement during elementary school, middle school, and high school? Was there a time period during which one or both parents were especially attuned or mis-attuned?

_____

_____

Give an example of a time when you were especially aware of your mother's attunement to you (or lack thereof).

_____

_____

_____

Give an example of a time when you were especially aware of your father's attunement to you (or lack thereof).

_____

_____

_____

2. **Responsiveness** refers to your parents' willingness to respond to you when you were distressed (mad, sad, afraid).

My mother:

_____ was responsive to me when I was mad. She was curious about why I was mad and invited me to talk about it.

_____ was responsive to me when I was sad. She was curious and offered comfort, care, and kindness.

_____ was responsive to me when I was afraid. She was curious and offered comfort, care, and kindness.

My father:

_____ was responsive to me when I was mad. He was curious about why I was mad and invited me to talk about it.

_____ was responsive to me when I was sad. He was curious and offered comfort, care, and kindness.

_____ was responsive to me when I was afraid. He was curious and offered comfort, care, and kindness.

How consistent was your parents' responsiveness during elementary school, middle school, and high school? Was there a time period during which one or both parents were especially responsive or unresponsive to you?

___

Give an example of a time when you were especially aware of your mother's responsiveness when you were mad, sad, or afraid (or a time when she was not responsive to you).

___

Give an example of a time when you were especially aware of your father's responsiveness when you were mad, sad, or afraid (or a time when he was not responsive to you).

___

3. **Engagement** refers to your parents' desire to truly know you, to pursue your heart.

_____ My mother had a genuine desire to really know me, and especially to know my heart. I felt pursued by her. I felt like she invited me to share my hopes, fears, dreams, and desires—but didn't require me to do this. There was space to share what I wanted to, but her pursuit did not feel invasive.

_____ My father had a genuine desire to really know me, and especially to know my heart. I felt pursued by him. I felt like he invited me to share my hopes, fears, dreams, and desires—but didn't require me to do this. There was space to share what I wanted to, but his pursuit did not feel invasive.

How consistent was your parents' engagement during elementary school, middle school, and high school? Was there a time period during which one or both parents were especially engaged or disengaged?

_____

_____

_____

Give an example of a time when you were especially aware of your mother's engagement of you (or lack thereof).

_____

_____

_____

Give an example of a time when you were especially aware of your father's engagement of you (or lack thereof).

_____

_____

_____

4. **Affect regulation** refers to your parents' ability and willingness to soothe you when you were anxious or scared and stimulate you when you were shut down.

_____ My mother was able to help me calm down when I was distressed or dysregulated (afraid, mad, sad, ashamed).

_____ My father was able to help me calm down when I was distressed or dysregulated (afraid, mad, sad, ashamed).

How consistent was your parents' ability and willingness to regulate your affect during elementary school, middle school, and high school? Was there a time period during which one or both parents were especially helpful or unhelpful with this?

_____

_____

Give an example of a time when you were especially aware of your mother's ability to soothe you when you were anxious or scared or stimulate you when you were shut down (or a time when she was not able to do this).

_____

_____

Give an example of a time when you were especially aware of your father's ability to soothe you when you were anxious or scared or stimulate you when you were shut down (or a time when he was not able to do this).

_____

_____

_____

5. **Strength to handle your big emotions** refers to the degree to which your parents welcomed your anger, sadness, and fear.

My mother:

_____ welcomed my anger. It was okay for me to be mad at Mom. I could say things like "I hate you" or "You're mean" or "You don't love me."

_____ welcomed my sadness. It was okay for me to cry and be sorrowful.

_____ welcomed my fear. It was okay for me to be afraid.

My father:

_____ welcomed my anger. It was okay for me to be mad at Dad. I could say things like "I hate you" or "You're mean" or "You don't love me."

_____ welcomed my sadness. It was okay for me to cry and be sorrowful.

_____ welcomed my fear. It was okay for me to be afraid.

Another component of a parent being strong enough to handle the child's big emotions is being able to regulate their own emotions without the child's assistance.

_____ Mom was able to regulate her own emotions. She did not need me to soothe her.

_____ Dad was able to regulate his own emotions. He did not need me to soothe him.

How consistent was your parents' willingness to welcome your big emotions during elementary school, middle school, and high school? Was there a time period during which one or both parents were especially able or unable to handle your big emotions?

Give an example of a time when you were especially aware of your mother welcoming your anger, sadness, and/or fear (or a time when she did not do this).

Give an example of a time when you were especially aware of your father welcoming your anger, sadness, and/or fear (or a time when he did not do this).

---

6. **Willingness to repair rupture** refers to your parents' willingness to own and rectify harm.

    _____My mother was aware when she said or did something that hurt me. She sought me out, acknowledged what she had done, apologized with a genuine "I'm sorry," reconnected with me, and attempted to repair the relational damage.

    _____My father was aware when he said or did something that hurt me. He sought me out, acknowledged what he had done, apologized with a genuine "I'm sorry," reconnected with me, and attempted to repair the relational damage.

How consistent was your parents' willingness to repair during elementary school, middle school, and high school? Was there a period of time during which one or both parents were especially willing or unwilling to repair?

_____

_____

_____

Give an example of a time when your mother owned and rectified harm she did to you.

_____

_____

_____

Give an example of a time when your father owned and rectified harm that he did to you.

_____

_____

_____

Now that you have completed this exercise, take a minute to check in with yourself. Check in with your *body*. As you've been thinking back on your relationship with your parents with regard to these six things, what have you been feeling in your body? Just notice that, whatever it is.

Look back on your responses. Securely attached people will score mostly fives (with an occasional four). If you scored lower than that, it means your developmental needs were not met as a child.

If your parents were not attuned, responsive, engaged, able to regulate your affect, strong enough to handle your big emotions, and willing to repair rupture, then your heart has been significantly wounded. You have experienced what's called developmental trauma, which occurs when the Big Six are not met in childhood.

5

INSECURE ATTACHMENT

Avoidant and Ambivalent Attachment

Your attachment style is more important than you may realize. Your attachment style refers to the particular way your brain has been primed to experience relationships in the present. As we learned in the last chapter, if your primary caregivers were sufficiently attuned, responsive, and engaged with you as a child, you developed what is called a *secure attachment*. There are also two primary types of *insecure attachment*: avoidant attachment and ambivalent attachment.[1]

AVOIDANT ATTACHMENT

When your caregiver is often unavailable, dismissive, or rejecting, you will develop an avoidant attachment.

Attachment is about feeling like your caregiver is there for you and responsive to you when you feel distressed (afraid, sad, mad). In the

---

1. There is a third category of insecure attachment, which is (unhelpfully) named disorganized attachment.

case of avoidant attachment, when the child becomes distressed, his caregiver does not provide sufficient comfort, care, and connection.[2] When the child tries to communicate his distress, his attempts have little to no effect on the parent. The child is forced to try to calm himself and regulate his own emotions.

The child's needs are frequently not met, and the child comes to believe that communicating his needs has no influence on the caregiver. An avoidantly attached child learns that it is more reliable to regulate his own anxiety than to seek comfort from his unavailable or unresponsive caregiver. The child comes to know that "Mom/Dad is going to dismiss me, misunderstand me, or make the situation worse. So, I guess I have to manage on my own."

For a child, few things are more frightening than realizing your parent is not attuned and responsive to you.

Eventually, the child learns it is fruitless to rely on others to meet his needs. Since his needs and wants rarely seem to matter to his caregiver, he soon stops trying to express what he needs and wants.

Reality, for this child, is quite simply: "I am alone and on my own."

As a result, the child becomes deeply self-reliant. He develops a view of himself as independent and strong because, after all, no one else is there to help him.

This child's experience in life has proven to his nervous system that *others aren't available*. The avoidant child does not *avoid* closeness to others; it simply isn't a menu option for him. *No one is there to attach to.*

Since his caregiver has proven to be emotionally unavailable, the avoidant child loses contact with the possibility of deep emotional connection to the point of not realizing that anything important is missing.

---

2. For ease of writing, I am using a male example throughout this section; however, both men and women can be avoidantly attached.

It is as if the neurological circuitry for connection is present but so disconnected that it prevents the development of a robust sense of relational hopes, desires, and longings.

How to Know If You Are Avoidantly Attached

As avoidantly attached children mature into adulthood, they tend to feel more comfortable with relational distance and separateness. Since emotional interdependence is so foreign, they manage their emotions independently from others. They may enjoy relationships but generally only let themselves rely on another when it is abundantly clear the other person will actually come through for them. This is because they were forced to adapt to the utter aloneness they experienced with their parents by relying on self-soothing and self-stimulation. In time, it became very difficult to turn to others.

Avoidantly attached adults are allergic to emotional interdependence—it feels dangerous to need others. When a partner offers or desires connection, the avoidant adult experiences some measure of fear or even panic. The sensation is similar to a numb limb that becomes painful when circulation is restored.

This, of course, often leaves their partners feeling lonely and emotionally disconnected from them. Avoidantly attached adults may feel relieved by—or excited by—brief or even extended separations. Their shift into autoregulation (versus turning to someone else for interactive regulation) is immediate and welcome.

Their bodies have been trained to not require another human being for regulation—because there never was another human being there to regulate them. They like being by themselves. They tend to rely on self-stimulating activities (watching TV, interacting with content on their smartphone, and so forth).

This can present a problem in intimate relationships. When interrupted by their partner, the avoidantly attached individual may feel like their partner is being intrusive.[3] Their subsequent rejection of their partner's approach is not meant to be cruel. They are simply trying to stay regulated. The result of this tendency toward self-regulation is that avoidantly attached adults require little interaction and rarely provoke overt interpersonal conflict.

For avoidantly attached people, emotional dysregulation usually doesn't look dysregulated. They may appear outwardly calm and project an aura of being unaffected, but inwardly they feel desperate to self-regulate and calm the relational storm around them.

Avoidantly attached adults tend to focus on the cerebral and analytical, avoiding the risk inherent in emotional connections with others. They like to keep a safe distance from their unmet attachment longings. As a result, they have decreased access to, and awareness of, their emotions.

They often feel needed but not really wanted, which also means they find true mutuality and inclusion foreign.

They will tend to recall facts about their life (such as where they lived, what school they attended, the make and model of their first car) but have great difficulty recalling memories of family experiences where there was authentic emotional engagement. They will often insist the past has little to no influence on their present life. But how can they know their family experiences had no impact on them if they cannot recall those family experiences? This is an example of the narrative incoherence that plagues avoidantly attached folks.

They also will tend to idealize their parents and minimize or downplay hurtful attachment experiences. Idealizing Mom and Dad allows the avoidantly attached individual to sidestep feeling the

---

3. Stan Tatkin, "Addiction to 'Alone Time'—Avoidant Attachment, Narcissism, and a One-Person Psychology within a Two-Person Psychological System," *The Therapist* 57 (January-February 2009), https://sonyathomaslcsw.com/wp-content/uploads/2015/12/Addiction-to-Alone-Time-Stan-Tatkin.pdf.

loneliness and emotional pain that resulted from being dismissed and/or rejected by one or both parents.

Avoidant Attachment: A Story

No two stories are alike. The story of each avoidantly attached adult is unique to that person. The following is simply one example illustrating the core dynamics that avoidantly attached folks grapple with and how past family of origin stories impact present life.

James came to see me on his thirty-fifth birthday. A tax accountant, he was married and trying to have children. James's stated reasons for beginning therapy included the following:

> "I want to be a better father to my son than my father was to me."
>
> "I have a hard time with emotions, and my wife is frustrated about how emotionally closed off I am."
>
> "I often feel anger toward my wife and wish that I wasn't so angry all the time. When I get angry, it feels like something in my chest is about to be unleashed, but then I immediately rein it in. I just shut it down."

When I asked James about his family of origin story, he said he couldn't remember much, either good or bad. A common response from James was "I just don't have many memories." However, he did have a few memories and, in time, the following pieces of data came out:

> James remembered playing air hockey as a four-year-old and badly hurting his finger on the edge of the air hockey table. There was a lot of blood, and it was very scary for him. However, as James told this story, he said, "Even though I remember Dad bandaging up my finger, I have no sense that my dad actually cared about me while he was putting the bandage on. It was more like he was a robot just doing

a task." When I asked James what it was like for him to tell me this story, he said, "I don't feel any anger; just a little sadness. Mostly, I feel numb."

James had a sister who was nine years older than him. When James was eight, he was outside playing on a jungle gym. He jumped down from a high platform, landed funny, and broke his ankle. James said that what he remembered most about this incident was how comforting it was to have his older sister there—caring for him and helping him. He doesn't remember his parents' involvement in this story in any way. But he vividly remembers how comforting it was to have his sister there. When I asked James, "Do you have any memories of feeling comforted by your mom or dad?" he replied, "I can't think of anything. They didn't really do that sort of thing."

By the time James was thirteen, his older sister had moved out of the house and lived across the neighborhood with her husband. A couple times a week after school, James would walk a mile to his sister's house because she was "much more helpful with my science homework than either of my parents."

When James was in high school, he spent most of his time alone in his room. He was frequently angry, and his dad accused him of "always being in your room, too angry at us to come out."

Finally, James said that most of his anger was focused on his dad because "Mom couldn't handle anything. If I expressed frustration to my mom, she would be deeply hurt and tell me I was being unfair. She was too fragile to handle my anger at her."

The most telling piece of data from the list above is James's response to my question, "Do you have any memories of feeling comforted by your mom or dad?" He said, "I can't think of anything. They didn't really do that sort of thing." The only source of comfort or safety for James was his older sister. James wept when he told me about walking the mile to his sister's house for help with his homework. His tears were about how kind and compassionate she was compared to his parents.

But how do these childhood stories shape James's present life? Let's make some linkages.

> Since James's feelings never mattered to his parents, his brain has been primed to assume there is no point expressing his feelings to his wife. She is not going to listen to his feelings or, if she does listen, she is not going to truly care about his feelings. This leaves his wife feeling like James is emotionally closed off and inaccessible to her. James feels shame that he is emotionally shut down and, at the same time, feels like if he expressed his feelings to his wife, she wouldn't care.

> When James is angry with his wife, he doesn't express the anger, because James's nervous system learned that other people will either reject him if he's too angry (like his dad did) or dissolve into a puddle of tears (like his mom did). In short, he has been primed to believe his anger is bad and will push people away from him. The dilemma, of course, is that James's wife can't validate and engage his anger if he refuses to express it to her.

> Self-contempt is a frequent companion for James. When I asked James to ponder why he would have spent so much time in his room seething with anger, he responded with, "I don't know why I was so angry, but my parents were right—nobody forced me to stay in my room. I did that on my own volition. No wonder I never had a good relationship with them." Instead of being curious about why he was so angry in high school, James turned on himself and joined his parents in their accusation that it was his fault

he didn't have a better relationship with them. The bind for James, however, was that if he came out of his room and expressed his anger, he would be shamed by his father and/or his mother would dissolve into tears. Since James did not want to see the cruelty of his parents, the only way he could make sense of his story was to say he was an angry kid who isolated himself from everyone. In other words, his loneliness was his fault. That's the self-contempt.

James was accustomed to being isolated and alone in his family of origin; therefore, he rarely initiated connection with his wife. His current relationship with her was a reenactment of his growing-up years—that is, James felt alone and isolated much of the time, just like he did as a boy.

When I invited James to ponder what it was like for him to rarely experience comfort from his parents, he responded by saying, "Well, my parents were always there. My dad even coached my soccer team from third grade until eighth grade. And, besides, I was the one who made the decision to stay in my room." When I pressed in about what it was like for him to feel so alone as a boy, he replied with, "Look, *I don't want to remember* how awful the loneliness was. I don't want to feel that stuff now. That takes me to a place I don't want to go." This is a very common response for an avoidantly attached adult who is being invited to feel their unfelt sadness, fear, and anger about their relationship with their primary caregivers.

AMBIVALENT ATTACHMENT

A child will develop an ambivalent attachment when she experiences her primary caregiver as inconsistent and, at times, intrusive.[4] When the child becomes distressed, the caregiver may—or may

---

[4] I am using a female example throughout this section; however, both women and men can be ambivalently attached.

not—provide soothing and comfort. It all depends on what is going on *for the caregiver* at that particular moment.

In other words, at times the parent is attuned and responsive to the child's needs but at other times is too preoccupied by their own emotional needs to focus on meeting the child's needs.[5] The child learns she cannot depend upon the parent to be attuned and responsive to her. Never knowing what to expect, the child develops a sense of anxiety and uncertainty about whether she can depend upon her caregiver or not.

This creates a sense that others cannot be relied upon to meet her needs. The child develops an inner franticness as she struggles to find relief from her anxiety and uncertainty. The parent's inconsistency and unreliability may not seem like a big deal when you think about it as an adult, but for a small child or infant, it is absolute terror.

As a result of this inconsistency, the child becomes hyperfocused on her caregiver—that is, the child attunes to the parent's emotional state rather than the parent attuning to the child's emotions. The relationship becomes primarily one in which the child is responding to the parent's emotional needs rather than vice versa.

This pattern of attachment essentially says, "I'm not certain whether my caregiver will be able to meet my needs, at least in any reliable way. Sometimes they can, and sometimes they can't. Which will it be this time?" Such anxiety creates a sense of uncertainty that others can't be relied upon to meet one's needs.

To make matters worse, ambivalently attached children often have at least one intrusive parent. *Intrusiveness* refers to the parent's

---

5. I know it sounds like I'm describing every single parent, since no parent is always attuned to their child. A child does not need perfect attunement. Ambivalent attachment is about the degree or frequency of a parent's responsiveness. And, ultimately, it is about the degree and frequency that parents notice there has been a relational rupture and seek to repair that rupture.

tendency to insert themselves into the child's world when the child is not inviting that. My mom was intrusive. She would walk across the house and give me a hug when I didn't actually want or need a hug. She would tell me things about her marriage to my dad that I didn't want to hear.

There was a season in which my dad would call home and tell my mom that he was going to miss dinner because he had to work late. My mom would make sure that I saw her heartbreak as she angrily took out a notebook and wrote down yet another date that Dad was working late. These kinds of interactions are intrusive—the child hasn't invited Mom to express her frustrations with Dad. It's unwanted closeness.

When I was a sophomore in high school, I was very upset because I felt like my dad cared way more about his work than he did about me or my brothers. I was expressing my sadness to my mom when she said, "Honey, you don't think your father is having an affair, do you?" This also was intrusive. I was not inviting Mom to talk to me about *her* fears.

The goal of intrusiveness is for the parent to get some of their adult relational needs met through their child. The child's heart becomes bound to the intrusive parent because the child knows that Mom or Dad needs them to be attuned, responsive, and engaged with their heartache and hurt. My mom needed me to tend to her because her husband was emotionally checked out of the marriage (for more on intrusiveness, see the discussion of triangulation in chapter 7).

How to Know If You Are Ambivalently Attached

As ambivalently attached children mature into adulthood, they will tend to experience intense emotions and have great difficulty regulating their anxiety. They will frequently feel an inner franticness as they struggle to find relief from their anxiety. When in distress, they often talk fast and erratically. They have difficulty editing what they are saying. Their speech may be hard to follow, overly emotional, and exaggerated.

Why is this the case? Because the ambivalently attached person *knows* that unless they dramatically express their pain, it is unlikely that another will respond. It's important to understand that this is not a cognitive belief. This is deep, body-based knowledge, rooted in their central nervous system. Their nervous system has learned that no one will respond unless they flail and amp up.

They will be plagued by a deep-seated fear they are going to be rejected or abandoned, which makes it very difficult to trust anyone. This leads to habitually seeking closeness (which their partner experiences as "clinging") and often asking for proof that they are loved. "Are you really there for me? Are you? Show me. Now show me again."

Ambivalently attached adults are always watching for relational disruptions, and they have a deep need for speedy resolution whenever there is relational rupture. This urgent/anxious need for repair and reconnection often pushes others away, thus creating a self-reinforcing feedback loop that says "Others are not dependable" and/or "I'm too much."

These folks anticipate relational rupture. They are primed for it. As a result, they feel a certainty within their body that hope leads to disappointment. In time, they become allergic to hope.[6]

Ambivalently attached adults often feel like the dynamics of their close relationships are unfair and unjust. The core cry of "That's not fair" is because it wasn't fair for them growing up—when their brain was learning how the world works. They tend to remember all of the unfair things that have transpired in the relationship, and they may need to talk through all the past wounds from their partner before making forward movement.

---

6. Stan Tatkin, "Allergic to Hope: Angry Resistant Attachment and a One-Person Psychology within a Two-Person Psychological System," *Psychotherapy in Australia* 18, no. 1 (November 2011): 66–73.

Ambivalently attached adults often feel like they are too "needy" and that they do not deserve to be loved in the way that they want. They suffer from self-criticism, insecurity, and a sense that something is wrong with them. They rely heavily on others to validate their self-worth, often seeking approval and reassurance from others. In intimate relationships, they will assume the role of the pursuer.

Ambivalent Attachment: A Story

Again, no two stories are alike. The story of each ambivalently attached adult is unique to that person. The following is simply one example illustrating the core dynamics ambivalently attached folks grapple with and how past family of origin stories impact present life.

When Cara entered my office, she stated three reasons for coming to therapy:

> "I'm dissatisfied in my marriage."
>
> "I'm very upset about how much I hurt my kids."
>
> "I think I might have some trauma in my past."

Cara remembered a fair number of stories from her growing-up years, and shared each of the following memories:

> Cara was very excited about returning to school to begin second grade. Her mom took her to Wal-Mart to buy clothes for the school year, but she hated the clothes her mom bought her. When she went to school, everyone made fun of her for her ugly outfit. After school she was crying in her room. When Cara told her mom what happened at school, she got angry at Cara for being so upset and said, "Cara, you're always taking things so seriously. You need to get thicker skin and learn to take a joke."

Cara's parents got divorced when she was entering high school. Sometimes, when it was her turn to be at Dad's, he would throw parties with his colleagues. After the guests arrived, Dad would "parade" her around, showing her off to everyone. When her dad introduced her, he would look at her in a "weird way." Cara said, "It was gross. It was like my dad was always assessing my body and loved showing me off to his friends. But these parties were the most attention I ever got from my dad (or my mom), and so part of me kind of liked the parties, even though it also felt weird and gross."

Cara vividly remembered chemistry class her junior year. Her mom was a chemistry teacher at another school, and she was excited about getting to spend time with her mom as she helped Cara with her chemistry homework, since that subject was her specialty. However, every time Cara got stuck on her chemistry homework and asked her mom for help, she'd say something like "Honey, I passed chemistry already. You need to figure it out on your own." Cara told me, "I was accustomed to Mom not helping me with other things, but I thought she would help me with chemistry because that was her area of expertise. I could never understand why Mom wouldn't even help me with something that she was so good at."

How do these childhood stories shape Cara's present life?

As a former college athlete, Cara loved watching college basketball. However, she complained that her husband "rarely accompanies me to my friends' houses to watch basketball . . . and when he does come, he just sits in the corner and doesn't say anything." For Cara, this experience is a reenactment of her experience in second grade with her ugly outfit. Cara's nervous system feels the same at these basketball parties as it felt when all the kids mocked her. It's the same bodily experience thirty years later.

Cara was triangulated by her father, which means that Cara's dad preferred Cara to Cara's mom. Cara's dad also sexualized his relationship with her. This set up Cara to be Mom's rival. Mom regularly made Cara pay for being the object of Dad's gaze. So, Cara's nervous system was constantly on guard to make sure men were not too attracted to her and to make sure women were not too envious of her. This is how her brain was primed to navigate the world: *make sure men are not too attracted to you because bad things happen when they are (think: Dad's parties) and make sure women are not too envious of you because bad things happen when they are (think: Mom's repeated cruelty, chemistry homework).*

Whenever we talked about her father, it was clear Cara had deep feelings for him. She was often defensive when asked to consider how his parties might have harmed her. In short, Cara was very loyal to her father. This makes sense in light of the fact that her father was the best thing in her world. Compared to how the cruelty of her mom made her feel, Cara's body felt good when she was with her father. Although Dad only provided a morsel of goodness, it seemed like a bountiful feast in comparison.

Cara is equally bound to her mother. When Cara's mom is cruel to her now, she brings it up and tries to talk to her mom about it. But Mom refuses to own her cruelty. As Cara puts it, "I can't stop going back to my mom and trying to get her to understand my point of view. But it never works. My mom has never once understood my heart when I've explained myself to her." Ambivalently attached adults often exert Herculean efforts to attempt to restore and reconcile broken relationships with people they care about. Cara has made sense of Mom's cruelty as "There must be something wrong with me" because no mother would treat her daughter this way.

Here's the key point: your attachment style (secure, ambivalent, or avoidant) profoundly affects how you experience relationships and how you express yourself in relationships. And your attachment style develops based on your relationships with your primary caregivers.[7]

> **Secure attachment** occurs when your primary caregivers are *often* attuned to you and often responsive to your needs and wants. Moreover, when there is relational rupture, the harm is quickly repaired. As a result, you feel seen, soothed, and safe again.
>
> **Ambivalent attachment** occurs when your primary caregivers are *sometimes* attuned to you and sometimes responsive to your needs and wants. At other times, your primary caregivers are preoccupied with their own anxieties, emotions, and moods.
>
> **Avoidant attachment** occurs when your primary caregivers are *rarely* attuned to you and rarely responsive to your needs and wants.

CHAPTER 5 KEY POINTS

- Avoidant attachment develops when caregivers are unavailable or dismissive, forcing the child to become emotionally self-reliant.
- Avoidantly attached adults tend to feel discomfort with emotional closeness and have a nervous system

---

7. Because experiences with each parent may be different, a child can be securely attached to one parent but insecurely attached to the other. See Siegel and Hartzell, *Parenting from the Inside Out*, 112.

predisposed to self-regulation rather than interactive regulation.
- Ambivalent attachment results from inconsistent caregiving interspersed with intrusiveness.
- Ambivalently attached individuals have great difficulty regulating their emotions, exhibit a fear of rejection, and have a heightened need for frequent emotional reassurance.

6

NAMING WHAT IS MOST TRUE ABOUT YOUR STORY

> Your memory is a monster; you forget—it doesn't. It simply files things away. It keeps things for you, or hides things from you—and summons them to your recall with a will of its own. You think you have a memory; but it has you!
>
> John Irving, *A Prayer for Owen Meany*

As you reflect on your story with regard to the Big Six, the next question that needs to be asked is the *why* question. If you realize your father was not attuned to you in middle school, the question is, Why? As you think about the dinner table night after night, if your mother was not responsive to your sad face, the question is, Why?

Please hear the next sentence loudly: ***there is always a why.***

There is always a why.

Humans are intentional creatures. Your parents are no exception.

Some of us believe our story is one of neglect. In my experience, neglect is rarely the truest thing about a person's story. Rarely. The question is, *Why* were you neglected?

My dad was not attuned to me when I was growing up. He was not responsive to me; he did not pursue me. He was preoccupied with his work. And when he wasn't focused on his work, he was outside taking care of his plants. The temptation for me is to make sense of my story as "Dad emotionally neglected me. He was a workaholic." And that is true. *It's just not what is most true.*

You will not experience freedom from the places where you are bound until you name what is most true about your story. In many ways, healing and growth are simply a matter of getting closer and closer to naming what is truest about your story.

As a boy, I had a deep longing for relationship with my father. Deep. I was always trying to position myself so he would talk to me, would ask me about my life and tell me about himself. However, even as a young boy, I was aware that my father was very distant from me.

And I never knew why.

I was a good kid. I obeyed my parents. I never got in trouble at school. I got good grades. I never could figure out, "Why didn't Dad like me?"

The answer is not as simple as "My dad just didn't do emotions. He didn't know how to relate to his sensitive son. He emotionally neglected me." If that is how I make sense of my story, there will be a ceiling on how much healing I experience.

Why? Because you cannot fully access grief and anger (both of which are necessary for healing) until you name what is most true about your story. So, I can put the question this way: "Why wasn't Dad fond of me?"

The answer? My dad was married to a woman—my mother. And this woman was more captivated by me than by her husband.

In other words, I was triangulated by my mother. *Triangulation*—which, again, I will explain in detail later—simply means that my mom looked to me for companionship and emotional connection rather than looking to her husband, my father.

My mom preferred me because, in many ways, I was a better husband to her than my father.

Now, here's the dilemma: What do you think it was like for my father to watch his wife choose me over him? It was emasculating and humiliating. And it (understandably) evoked envy in him. My dad was envious of me. This explains why my dad was not fond of me and explains my lifelong, largely unfulfilled quest of trying to find deeper connection and intimacy with my dad. I finally understood the *why* of my dad's "neglect."

As you start to see some of the ways your parents harmed you during your growing-up years, you will likely feel pressure to explain that harm in any way other than "They did it on purpose."

When I began to let in the fact that my mom made me her surrogate spouse, every fiber of my being screamed, "Okay, but I don't think she did it *on purpose*. She was doing the best she could given her history and circumstances."

Let me say at the outset that there is such a thing as unintentional harm. Was some of the harm you experienced unintentional? Absolutely. You have experienced both unintentional harm and intentional harm. But it's very important to be clear about which was which.

Why? Because your story is not going to make sense until you are honest and truthful about the intentional harm you experienced in your family of origin.

MIND MAPPING

In 2019, therapist David Schnarch wrote a very helpful book called *Brain Talk* in which he pointed out that all human beings have an ability called mind mapping.

Mind mapping refers to mapping out the thoughts and feelings of another person, such as your mother or father. You are able to map out—to know—something of the thoughts and feelings of others as they interact with you.

For example, when five-year-old you spilled your milk, and your father screamed at you, your brain had the ability to realize, *Dad is mad at me for spilling my milk*. You've mind mapped your father.

Suppose some of your spilled milk rolls off the table and onto Mom's lap. You look at Dad, and as you do, you are continuing to map his thoughts and emotions. *Dad is even more angry now ... because the milk got on Mom's new dress.*

Then Mom starts crying because her sister is coming over later, and Mom is always comparing her appearance to her sister's appearance—and now Mom can't wear the dress she looks best in. Of course, Dad is also aware of this, and so now Dad is even more upset.

Your mind—even as a five-year-old—has the ability to know all of that information. That's mind mapping in action. By reading your father's facial expression and tone of voice, your brain has mapped out a rather complex explanation for why Dad is so upset.

And, by the way, how do you know that Mom feels insecure around her sister? Because you map Mom's mind when her sister comes to visit. Mind mapping is a very powerful ability of your brain.

We mind map each other all the time.

Here's another example: suppose your father was a violent man who would lash out at you as a kid whenever he got upset. You would have become very skilled at mapping him so that you could anticipate his next explosion.

I listen to clients tell me stories of harm all the time. And when I ask them, "What was your father thinking and feeling when he said that cruel thing to you?" very often my clients say they don't know.

It's like they have a gap in their memory or their mind mapping ability suddenly shut off.

For example, suppose you tell me a story about coming downstairs after getting ready for junior prom.

You spent a long time in the bathroom with your hair and makeup, and as you come down the stairs, your father sees you and says, "Wow, you look stunning, young lady . . . better than your mother has ever looked." After I hear this story, I ask you, "What was your father's facial expression as he said this?" And all you can say is, "It was weird."

I then ask a more disturbing question. "What do you think your father was thinking and feeling about you as he said 'You look stunning, young lady . . . better than your mother has ever looked'?"

You respond, "I don't know what he was thinking or feeling. It was weird." Now, what's going on? Why did your mind mapping ability go offline? Why can't you map your father's mind in that moment? Because of traumatic mind mapping.

Traumatic mind mapping is a collapse of your brain's normal abilities that occurs when you are mind mapping someone and what you see is *terrible*.

It's so terrible your brain's abilities become impaired. You get what Schnarch calls "spaghetti brain." Traumatic mind mapping (spaghetti brain) happens when you realize someone close to you *is intentionally trying to hurt you*.

When someone close to you (like your father) is intentionally trying to hurt you—for example, by sexualizing you—the mind mapping ability of your brain stops working.

Here's how Schnarch puts it:

> When we think someone is deliberately trying to hurt us, it blows our mind and our mind mapping ability shuts down. . . . Rather

than deal with it directly, we prefer to keep ourselves in a gray area *where we remain unsure of that person's true motivations.* . . . We get spaghetti brain.[1]

Instead of letting in the reality that your parent is deliberately trying to hurt you, you *pretend you don't really know their true motivations.* This is spaghetti brain. Your mind mapping ability goes offline because what you are seeing is too awful to bear.

Now, fast-forward twenty years after junior prom. You tell a different therapist—not me—the story of what your dad said as you were coming down the stairs. And your therapist responds by saying, "It doesn't sound like your father was trying to hurt you; he probably just lacked empathy—he probably didn't realize the impact his words and actions were having on you."

This therapist's point is that your dad didn't realize he was making you feel uncomfortable, and you would likely want to agree. If you've ever reflected on times when you were mistreated by your parents, you have probably tried to make sense of the experience as "They just didn't know they were hurting me so much."

Here's the problem with this explanation: *it assumes your parents don't have mind mapping ability themselves.*

To say "Dad just lacked empathy, and he didn't realize the impact of his words on me" assumes that your dad didn't have the ability to know how his words would affect teenage you.

But of course he knew how this was going to make you feel.

Of course he knew this was going to make you feel uncomfortable.

Of course he knew you were going to feel creeped out by his sexually suggestive comment.

---

1. David Schnarch, *Brain Talk: How Mind Mapping Brain Science Can Change Your Life & Everyone in It* (Evergreen, CO: Sterling Publishers, 2019), 112. Emphasis mine.

Of course he knew this was going to make you feel like you were in competition with your own mother.

How did he know this? Because he has mind mapping ability. Just like you were able to map his mind as a five-year-old when you spilled your milk, he was able to map your mind as you were walking down the stairs. He knew you were hoping for your father to delight in your beauty in an honoring way without sexualizing you ... and without comparing you to your mother. He knew this.

And he also knew that, as the words came out of his mouth, you felt creepy feelings in your body. How did he know that? Because he could read your facial expression and body language.

Your father—just like you—has mind mapping ability.

His brain works.

Now, why do we tend to assume that the people who harmed us didn't mean to do it on purpose? Because it's easier on our brains!

You don't want to believe your father said and did those things on purpose. And so you assume he wasn't aware of how his comments would impact you.

Empathy is the human capacity to know and understand another person's emotions and thoughts. I use the terms *empathy* and *mind mapping* interchangeably. In our culture, when people speak of empathy they usually mean compassion. But *compassion is different from empathy*. Compassion is concern for another person's suffering.

Here's what you have to understand: *it is absolutely possible to have empathy without compassion.*

The father in the junior prom story had loads of empathy but no compassion. He was a cruel man, but he had plenty of empathy. In other words, he knew what his daughter was feeling (empathy) without having any concern for what she was feeling (compassion).

Another example of empathy without compassion is bullying. The only way to skillfully mock and humiliate another kid is to know what that other kid is thinking and feeling. Good bullies excel at picking out the sensitive kids and the kids who won't fight back. How can they be so good at knowing which kids to bully and which kids to leave alone? Because good bullies are deeply empathetic; they are skilled at reading the thoughts and feelings of others.

> *What about just identifying the weak*

The idea that *My parents didn't mean to hurt me* can only be true if your parents lacked the ability to mind map you. There is an alternative explanation, however. You may have stories in which your parents mind mapped you very well... and used their knowledge of your thoughts and feelings to hurt you more deeply.

Consider the following example.

> Jim is a fourteen-year-old boy who is not very good at sports or academics. But this year Jim really takes a liking to art class and realizes he has some artistic abilities. While Jim and his mom are at the mall, they wander into an art store and see a landscape watercolor painting that Jim absolutely loves. Jim says to his mom, "I think I'm going to buy that painting."
>
> And Mom looks right at Jim and contemptuously says, "Why would you waste your hard-earned money on a worthless painting? Artists are just dreamers who can't hold down a real job."

Thirty years later, Jim is in therapy talking about this story, and Jim's therapist says, "Perhaps your mom wasn't a very empathetic person. She probably didn't realize how much her comment hurt you."

Here's an alternative explanation: Jim's mom had lots of empathy, and she used her empathy to craft a comment that would be especially painful to Jim. Mom's ability to mind map Jim—that is, to know Jim was developing a love for art—is precisely how Mom got the information she used to make her comment sting more deeply.

There are two kinds of empathy. First is *compassionate empathy*, in which you mind map someone, realize what they are feeling and thinking, and feel care and concern for their pain.

And then there is *antisocial empathy*, a term coined by Schnarch, in which you mind map someone, realize what they are feeling and thinking, and use that information to wound them.[2] *Antisocial empathy* is what happens when you mind map someone and then use that information to hurt them. Bullies have antisocial empathy.

Here's the point: healing requires constructing an accurate understanding of your autobiographical narrative. Currently, you likely have *gaps* in your stories. Those gaps include places where your brain collapsed because of traumatic mind mapping. Remember, traumatic mind mapping leads to "spaghetti brain"—it is the failing of your brain's mind mapping abilities that occurs when you are experiencing intentional harm from someone emotionally close to you, like a parent.

When someone close to you hurts you on purpose, you get overwhelmed by big emotions—especially when you are a child or adolescent. When your brain is flooded with big emotions, certain portions of your brain shut down. This is why you have a hard time remembering the look on your parent's face or their tone of voice.

As Schnarch points out, when you get spaghetti brain you become fooled into believing that your father or mother doesn't know what they are doing.[3] Why? Because it's too overwhelming to let yourself see the truth.

Think back to being that girl coming down the stairs for junior prom. When your father said, "You look stunning, young lady . . . better than your mother has ever looked," you had what's called a "disgust reaction" in your brain.

---

2. Schnarch, *Brain Talk*, 138.
3. Schnarch, *Brain Talk*, 112–15.

You were repulsed by your father's words and by his creepy facial expression and aroused tone of voice. When you had this disgust reaction, your mind mapping system stopped working. In other words, you lost the ability to know that your father was sexualizing you *on purpose*.

Your brain was not able to process this piece of information. Therefore, when you recorded the event in your autobiographical memory, you omitted the part about how Dad was aroused by you. You also omitted the part about the enjoyment on Dad's face when he compared you to Mom.

As a result, you now have a gap in your memory. And that gap is the *intentionality* behind your father's words. Decades later, when you recall this event, you will not be able to recall the map of your father's mind. And so, when I ask you, "What do you think your father was thinking and feeling as he said those words to you?" you'll respond with "I don't know." You're not lying. Nor do you have a bad memory. Your brain was simply traumatized.

You may have had a therapist (or a friend) tell you that your abusive caregiver didn't really mean to hurt you. These words are meant to be comforting; however, they will keep you stuck. They will block your healing process. Why? Because you won't develop an accurate picture of your story. Healing requires that you understand *what really went down*.

The purpose of naming intentionality—the purpose of realizing that your parent really meant to do it—is so that you can heal.

IMPLICIT MEMORY: THE KEEPER OF YOUR STORIES

Memory is the way in which a past experience affects how the mind will function in the present. In other words, your memory influences your present day-to-day life—and then some. Memory *shapes* your present. Deeply. If memory is the way in which past experiences affect how your mind will function later this afternoon, wouldn't it be wise to know as much as possible about your past experiences?

There are two layers of memory: implicit and explicit. Explicit memory is what we tend to think of when we hear the word *memory*. If I asked you to think of your first grade teacher, you would use explicit memory to access that information. Explicit memory is important. But implicit memory is *vastly* more important when it comes to how we actually live our lives.

The ability to create explicit memories does not develop until approximately twenty-four months of age, but implicit memory is operational before you come out of the womb. Everything you learn in the first two years of life is recorded in implicit—not explicit—memory.

To record something in explicit memory, you have to be *paying attention*. If you want to remember that the capital of New York is Albany, you have to be paying attention when you are studying the state capitals. However, implicit memories are created *whether you are paying attention or not.*

Implicit memories are recorded without your awareness. **Without you paying attention.**

You don't think to yourself, *I need to remember this.* When it comes to implicit memory, you just remember it automatically, without realizing that you are recording a memory at all.

For the first two years of your life—when you were completely dependent on your parents for everything—every experience you had was encoded in implicit memory. The brain is not able to record explicit memories until around twenty-four months of age (which is why you don't "remember" anything from when you were an infant). I put remember in quotations because, far from not remembering anything from your first two years of life, you actually remember everything. Without trying to. It's just that your experiences in the first two years of life are recorded in implicit—not explicit—memory.

The second thing to know about implicit memory is that when you recall an implicit memory today, you don't experience *the sensation that you are remembering something*.

Please read that sentence again.

It is hard to overstate the importance of this fact.

If I asked you, "Who was your first grade teacher?" you would try to recall your teacher's name and face. As you thought back to first grade, you would have a sensation in your body telling you, "I'm thinking back in time and remembering something." This is called the sensation of recall. This sensation always accompanies the retrieval of an explicit memory (like your first grade teacher, sixteenth birthday party, or high school graduation).

However, when you retrieve an implicit memory, *there is no sensation of recall*. You don't have that sense you are remembering something. In other words, when you remember an implicit memory, you are not aware you are remembering something from the past. ***It feels present.***

Here's an example: suppose you and your friend are walking in the park, and a cocker spaniel starts racing toward you. Immediately, your body floods with fear. However, you have no sense of *Oh, this is because I'm remembering that I was attacked by a dog when I was five*. Yet that implicit memory is precisely what is causing your body to feel fear.

Your friend, who had a friendly dog growing up, has a very different reaction. Without feeling any fear at all, she bends down on one knee and opens her arms to hug the incoming cocker spaniel.

Now, why do the two of you have such different reactions to the exact same event? Implicit memory.

Your friend's implicit memory informed her that dogs are friendly and fun while yours informed you that they are dangerous and frightening.

Dan Siegel explains, "The brain is an anticipation machine that shapes ongoing perception by what it automatically expects based on prior experience."[4]

One reason your past story matters so much is because your brain will experience whatever happens this afternoon *through the lens of your past story.*

MONET AND VAN GOGH

If you were an art history major in college, and today you are presented with two paintings you had never seen—one a Monet and one a van Gogh—you would immediately be able to tell which was which. Now, how could you possibly know that a particular painting was a van Gogh if you had never seen that specific painting before? Implicit memory.

As you look at both paintings, you unconsciously and automatically remember all the van Gogh paintings you've seen over the course of your life. These implicit memories tell you what a van Gogh *feels* like. Implicit memory is about the "feel" of things.

Suppose that for the first eighteen years of your life, every painting you saw was painted by van Gogh. You never saw any abstract paintings, or realist paintings, or modernist paintings—just van Gogh. As an eighteen-year-old, you wouldn't think *This is what a van Gogh looks like* but rather *This is what* paintings *look like.*

This is precisely what happens with your understanding of—and expectations for—relationships. Your brain summarizes all your experiences of relating with your mother, and instead of thinking *This is what a relationship with* my mom *is like*, you think *This is what* relationships *are like.*

---

4. Daniel Siegel, *The Mindful Therapist: A Clinician's Guide to Mindsight and Neural Integration* (New York: W. W. Norton, 2010), 35.

Curt's story is another example to illustrate how an implicit memory from the past profoundly affects present life.

Curt burst into tears midway through our couple's counseling session. His wife, Jennifer, had just expressed how angry she was because Curt's anxiety had sidelined him from the family for an entire Saturday. I asked Curt what it felt like for him to hear this from his wife.

He replied, "I feel emasculated and humiliated. . . . I feel like a boy instead of a man."

I asked Curt where he felt that sense in his body. He located it in his chest and gut.

Then I said, "Just notice that sensation of emasculation and humiliation in your chest and gut. Now, think back on your life . . . have you ever felt that feeling before?"

Curt immediately began crying and said, "Yes, yes. When I was twelve. I was on the phone with my dad. We had just moved from California to Texas, but my dad had to stay back in California for three months. I was the oldest of three kids, and I was supposed to be helping my mom hold everything together while my dad was still in California working. But I was so upset about moving away from my friends, and I felt incredibly anxious in our new neighborhood where I didn't know anyone. Instead of taking care of my mom and sisters, I would sit in my room filled with anxiety. My dad said to me over the phone, 'You're supposed to be the man of the house right now. You're supposed to be taking care of your mom and sisters. Instead you're alone in your room nursing your stupid feelings.' And then he hung up. I just sat there feeling humiliated and emasculated. I so wanted to be able to do what my dad asked, but I couldn't."

Let's take a look at how Curt's implicit memory from the past is influencing his present emotional experience with his wife.

Jennifer was angry because Curt's anxiety isolated him from the family. When Jennifer expressed her anger about this—when she told Curt specifically why she was angry at him—Curt immediately began having a very painful reaction in his body. He felt the bodily sensations associated with emasculation and humiliation. Now, *the question is why.*

Why? Because our past experiences—stored in implicit memory—intrude in the present and activate bodily sensations in the present.

In this case, Curt remembered the time when his father angrily shamed him for being sidelined in his room "nursing his stupid feelings" instead of taking care of his mother and sisters. However, because this experience was stored in *implicit* rather than explicit memory, Curt *had no sensation of recall* as he was sitting in my office. He had no idea he was remembering something. As a result, he had no idea why he was so upset by Jennifer's anger.

It's important to understand that as Jennifer expressed anger at Curt for not being able to overcome his anxiety, Curt felt very similar feelings in the present to what he felt that day in his bedroom as a twelve-year-old. *This is because his brain was remembering something.* But since the emotions and bodily sensations he experienced as a twelve-year-old were recorded in implicit memory, Curt had no sensation of recall.

Therefore, *Curt had no idea he was remembering anything at all.*

This led to profound confusion about why he felt emasculated when his wife expressed anger at him for being debilitated with anxiety.

When we leave home and set out into the world, we carry within us a storehouse of implicit memories. *And those implicit memories tell us what to expect around every bend.*

We continue to record implicit memories throughout our lives, but experiences in adulthood wield a much weaker influence on the brain. Childhood experiences create the foundation of the brain, and later experiences merely make adjustments to that foundation.

Here's how Dan Siegel puts it:

> Implicit memories cause us to form expectations about the way the world works, based on our previous experiences.... Implicit memory creates something called "priming" in which *the brain readies itself to respond in a certain way.*[5]

"OVERREACTIONS"

Do you ever feel intense emotions that you know are "more than the situation calls for"? Perhaps you think these experiences are overreactions. For example, someone asks you a seemingly innocuous question, and abruptly you feel enraged, or panicked, or ashamed.

What if these intense emotional reactions are not overreactions at all?

What if they are directly proportional to how your brain receives the other person's communication and interprets their words and tone of voice *through the grid of your implicit memory*?

Something in the other person's tone of voice or facial expression or choice of words has called to mind memories of deeply significant past experiences.

And you are remembering those experiences, but because those experiences are stored in implicit memory, you are not aware you are remembering anything at all. It's not that you are "too sensitive" or a "drama queen." You simply have a brain with a treasure trove of implicit memories.

---

5. Daniel Siegel and Tina Payne Bryson, *The Whole Brain Child* (New York: Random House, 2012), 72. Emphasis mine.

Situations that evoke strong emotional responses make implicit memory known. To say it differently, situations that evoke strong emotional responses in you *tell you something about your story*.

There is a reason you feel the deep feelings you do. There is a reason you fly off the handle when you do. There is a reason your heart starts to race in the middle of certain conversations/fights/arguments. And those reasons will be found buried (not so deeply) in your stories.

CHAPTER 6 KEY POINTS

- An important part of making sense of your story is identifying the *why* behind the relational dynamics in your family of origin.
- Human beings—including your primary caregivers—are intentional creatures. We all have wills.
- *Mind mapping* refers to mapping out the thoughts and feelings of another person.
- Traumatic mind mapping (spaghetti brain) happens when you realize someone close to you is intentionally trying to hurt you.
- It is absolutely possible to have empathy without compassion.
- Big emotional reactions in the present are almost always tied to past experiences stored in implicit memory.

7

WHAT IF YOU ENGAGED YOUR SEXUAL STORY?

> Sexual brokenness pinpoints the location of our past harm.
> Jay Stringer, *Unwanted*

When I was thirty-five years old, I didn't think I had a story. I would have told you that my dad was sometimes emotionally and physically harmful, but that would have been it. I had not written out any of my stories. If you had asked me, "Were you sexually abused?" I would have responded with a resounding "No, of course not." However, my life was very painful. In other words, *I had symptoms*. Fear, anxiety, dread, depression. My nervous system was frequently dysregulated, making relationships difficult.

When you experience symptoms like these and don't think you have a story that can account for the symptoms, you sometimes feel crazy. I certainly did. I felt like there was something drastically wrong with me. Why? Because *I had all these emotional problems and no explanation for them.*

As I mentioned in chapter 1, it was around this time that someone gave me a copy of *The Wounded Heart* by Dan Allender. I don't know why I started reading it, because the subtitle of the book is *Hope for Adult Victims of Childhood Sexual Abuse*, and I had not been sexually abused.

Yet as soon as I began reading, I found myself in the pages. I had never read a book that more accurately depicted the landscape of my heart. But all the talk about sexual abuse was grating. In order to get through it, I took a black permanent marker, and every time I came across the term "sexual abuse," I crossed out the word *sexual*.

After finishing *The Wounded Heart*, I heard about a weeklong group experience that was run by Dan called Recovery Week. So I flew to Seattle to be with this man, the author of the book that was finally giving me words for my internal experience. There were ten men at my Recovery Week, and we were placed into two groups. Each man was invited to take twenty-five minutes to tell his story. I spent twenty-three minutes talking about the abuse from my dad—the emotional, verbal, and physical harm. I used the last two minutes to say the following: "My mom and I were pretty close. We were the two most emotional members of our family, and we had a close emotional bond. I guess in some ways I was like my mom's surrogate spouse since my dad was so emotionally checked out of their marriage."

When I was done speaking, Dan said to the group, "Does anyone have any questions for Adam?" His words irritated me, to put it lightly. I had not flown across the country to hear from other men who were just as lost and confused as I was. I only wanted to hear from Dan.

One of the men in my group responded to Dan's invitation by asking me, "Do you think your father was jealous of your relationship with your mother?" My reflexive response was to blow him off. I said, "I don't know. I guess. Sure."

And then came the moment that changed my life.

Dan looked at me, leaned forward in his chair a little bit, and simply said, *"Do you really want that to be your answer?"*

I can't explain what happened next, except to say that a shudder went through my body. Dan was inviting me to see something I had been unaware of for thirty-five years. That moment changed my life. To this day, I date my life from before and after that moment. That was the beginning of naming that my mother's relationship with me included sexual harm.

THE SEXUAL FANTASIES OF A SIX-YEAR-OLD

My earliest memories of sexuality occurred when I was six. I remember lying on my bed at night fantasizing about Mrs. Heidenreich and Mrs. McPherson. They were the mothers of two of my friends. Mrs. Heidenreich lived across the street, and Mrs. McPherson lived four doors down. As a six-year-old, I had very little knowledge of the mechanics of sex. Therefore, my fantasies did not involve intercourse, but they were decidedly sexual nonetheless. I would imagine myself sitting up in bed next to Mrs. McPherson and leaning over and kissing her. It was heavenly. This fantasy soothed me to sleep many nights.

I was also six the first time I let myself express sexual desire to an actual person. One day I nervously dialed Mrs. Heidenreich's phone number. When she answered the phone, I quickly spoke into the receiver, "I love you," and hung up. My little heart was pounding. But I did it! I told Mrs. Heidenreich that I loved her. Warm, electric feelings of arousal pulsed through my body.

Why am I telling you about my sexual fantasies as a six-year-old? Why am I telling you a portion of my story that lasted no more than thirty seconds? Because these seemingly insignificant anecdotes are precious pieces of data. Taken together, they hint at the reality of what had happened to that young boy by age six.

Exploring your story is a lot like detective work. Detectives collect sufficient data so they can piece together the scene of a crime. The data tell the truth of what really happened. Similarly, exploring your story is about mining your memory for clues about what really happened to you as a boy or girl. When you collect the clues—the data points—they will tell the truth. The truth of the story of your life.

Initially, my memories of having sexual fantasies about Mrs. Heidenreich and Mrs. McPherson held immense shame for adult me. *What kind of six-year-old does that?!* I thought. However, today these memories are sacred and precious to me. Why? Because they tell the truth about what happened!

As ironic as it may be, here is an axiom of story work: *the memories that hold the deepest shame for you will be the very memories that can set you free.*

What kind of six-year-old has sexual fantasies about two mothers on his street?

This is an excellent question *if it is allowed to be a question*. However, for me it had been an accusation. Until I was willing to ponder it as a question, I couldn't uncover the truth of my story. What kind of six-year-old has sexual fantasies about other moms? The kind who has been repeatedly sexualized and aroused by his own mother.

You, too, have borne the weight of accusations. Behind each experience of shame is an accusation. What if the accusations that haunt you could become questions you explore with curiosity and kindness?

WHAT AROUSES YOU?

When I was a senior in high school, some of my classmates dated sophomore girls. I remember thinking, *Who in the world would date someone younger than them?* It made absolutely no sense to me. I had no arousal for anyone younger than me. Why? Because my brain had been conditioned to be aroused by older women (like my mother), not younger women.

You are aroused by particular things in the present because of your experiences of being aroused in the past.

Have you noticed that not everyone is turned on by the same things? There is a reason for this. Your past story can help you understand why you are turned on by certain things. Your sexual preferences and sexual fantasies *are not random.*

As counselor Jay Stringer points out in *Unwanted,* when it comes to your sexual story, there are always two storylines at play.[1] There is the storyline of your present sexual struggles, and then there is the storyline of your growing-up experiences that *set you up* for those present sexual struggles.[2] In the language of Isaiah (Isaiah 61:1), there is the storyline of your present captivities, and then there is the storyline of where your heart was broken as a boy or girl.

There is always a linkage between your wounding and your bondage/captivity. There is a connection between your painful experiences growing up and your present sexual life. Take any present-day sexual struggle: previous scenes from your story will illuminate its origins. Sexual harm in the past becomes reenacted in the present. This is because you have neurons... and that's how neurons operate.

Your brain is an anticipation machine: it operates on the principle of priming. *Priming* simply means your brain anticipates what will come next *based on past experiences.*

---

1. Jay Stringer, *Unwanted: How Sexual Brokenness Reveals Our Way to Healing* (Colorado Springs: NavPress, 2018).

2. I am not saying that your present sexual life is fully explainable by your family of origin experiences. Many other factors affected your sexual development, including evangelical purity culture, peer group experiences, teachers/mentors, and the media.

What if you became curious about what arouses you? What if you brought some genuine curiosity to the specific ways in which your present sexual brokenness may have grown out of past sexual harm?

For example, there is no such thing as someone who "struggles with pornography." You struggle with *particular kinds* of pornography. You are aroused by this type of person doing this particular thing, and you are *not* aroused by that type of person doing that particular thing. Can you bring some curiosity to why you are aroused by *this* and not *that*? Answering these kinds of questions will introduce you to parts of your sexual story you may not be aware of yet.

Perhaps there is a method to the madness, a very reasonable explanation as to why your sexuality plays out the way it does. If you are married, you likely fight with your spouse about sex and/or sex seems more complicated than it should be. What if these fights or complications are best understood as the inevitable conflict between your childhood story and your spouse's childhood story? And what if understanding your family of origin story can help you make sense of the madness in your marriage?

EVERYONE'S SEXUAL STORY IS FRAUGHT

Virtually no one makes it to adulthood without experiencing some form of sexual harm. This is because God loves sex, and as a result, the kingdom of evil despises your sexuality. Said another way, your sexuality has been strategically assaulted so that your sexual freedom and pleasure will be diminished.

The primary way evil assaults your sexuality is through the introduction of sexual shame. Shame is the bodily sense that there is something wrong with us, and therefore we are undesirable to others. Sexual shame creates the internal sense of *If others knew this about me, they would not want to be in relationship with me.*

What sexual shame do you carry? Do you have any sexual desires or fantasies you are ashamed of? How long have you felt ashamed of those desires/fantasies?

There is no way to engage your *past* sexual story without entering terrain that is replete with shame, confusion, and some measure of harm. And there is no way to engage your *present* sexual story without entering terrain that is replete with unmet longing, deep disappointment, and a war with hope.

The invitation to explore your sexual story is an invitation to go where angels fear to tread. However, if God intends for you to experience overflowing sexual pleasure and lavish sexual freedom, then exploring your sexual story is more than worth it.

So, here are some questions to begin with:

> How did you come to learn about sex? Was your introduction to sexuality via television, movies, older kids in the neighborhood, pornography, a health class at school?
>
> Did your parents ever give you the "sex talk"? If so, what was that like for you?
>
> What is the story around getting your period? Who guided you through that formative coming-of-age experience?
>
> How did your parents respond to your developing body? What did they say or not say about your body?
>
> How did your parents feel about your boyfriends/girlfriends?

Just as everyone's sexual story is fraught, everyone's sexual story is also unique. *What is yours?* If you can, take some time to write a one-page narrative answering the following three questions:

1. How did you first learn about sex and sexuality?
2. How have you experienced sexual harm?
3. What specifically do you feel sexual shame about?

SEXUAL ABUSE

Everyone has experienced some form of sexual harm. However, sadly, for many of us, the sexual harm we experienced is properly termed *sexual abuse*.

As Dan Allender points out in his landmark book *The Wounded Heart*, sexual abuse comes in two forms: sexual contact and sexual interactions.[3] Sexual contact refers to *physical touch* that is intended to arouse sexual desire in either the perpetrator or the victim. Sexual interactions, on the other hand, refer to sexual violations that do not involve physical touch. Most people are aware that inappropriate sexual contact constitutes sexual abuse. But it can be much harder to name the violation of inappropriate sexual *interactions*. Examples of sexual interactions that are abusive include:

> One of your parents walked through the house in their underwear.
>
> Your father made comments about your developing body in your presence.
>
> Your mother told you about her marital frustrations with your father, sometimes even mentioning her sexual disappointment.
>
> Your father left his pornographic magazines where you could find them.[4]

Whether the sexual abuse you experienced falls into the category of sexual contact or sexual interactions, the damage to your heart, mind, and body is *severe*. The primary damage from sexual abuse can best be described in one word: *complicity*.

---

[3]. Dan Allender, *The Wounded Heart*, rev. ed. (Colorado Springs: NavPress, 2008), 48.
[4]. For a more in-depth explanation of these categories, please see Allender, *Wounded Heart*, 49–52.

The word *complicit* means to be involved with another in wrongdoing. I am in no way saying that the abuse was your fault. However, the hard truth needs to be named: the goal of evil in sexually abusing you is to torment you with the awareness of your own complicity in the midst of the horror. Indeed, shame takes root in our hearts through the body-based knowledge that we were complicit in our own sexual abuse.

When you think back on your abuse, you may feel complicit in one—or all four—of the following ways:

1. I was complicit in that I desired the kindness and attention of the person who abused me. I enjoyed being with my abuser at times.
2. I was complicit in that I had some measure of choice when I went into the abusive situation . . . *and I chose to go*. Very often, this involves the agonizing reality of receiving something good in exchange for being abused. In other words, I was willing to pay the price of abuse in order to get something good from my relationship with my abuser.
3. I was complicit in that—at some point during the abuse—I stopped resisting. I stopped saying no; I stopped fighting.
4. I was complicit in that my body responded with some measure of arousal during the abuse.

Simply put, complicity refers to the knowledge that *I did something to participate in the abuse*. And right around the bend from that sentence is this accusation: *I wanted it. If I'm honest with myself, part of me wanted it.*

There is truth in the accusation—but it's not the full truth. The full truth can best be summarized as *No, I didn't want to be abused. But* hell yes *I wanted what I thought was genuine attention, affection, connection, care, and kindness that my abuser wove into our relationship.*

More than anything else, healing from sexual abuse is about blessing *the goodness of your desire* for attention, affection, connection, care, and kindness while also grieving that the cost of this desire was so very high.

TRIANGULATION

When it comes to understanding your sexual story, it is important to understand the relational dynamics between you, your parents, and any siblings. The reason for this will become clear.

One of the things we all need to do at some point is draw a triangle. Label the triangle points Mom, Dad, and You.[5] The closeness of the points of the triangle should represent the emotional closeness of the relationships. Thus, in the triangle below, Mom and Dad are emotionally closer to one another than either one of them is to You, the child:

Figure 7.1

Triangulation Parents

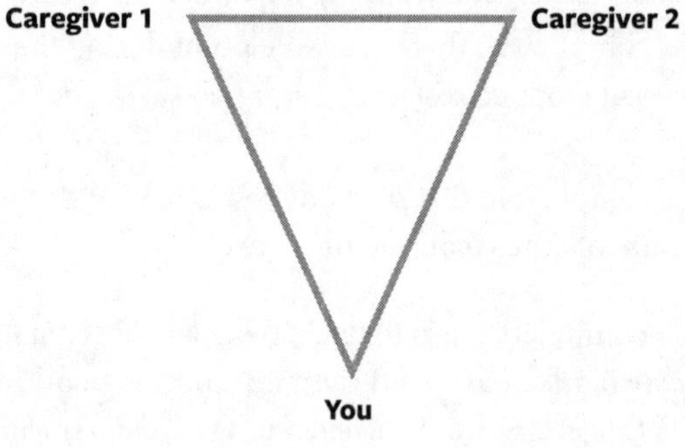

Caregiver 1   **Caregiver 2**

You

When this is the case, the foundation is set for you to develop a secure attachment. Sadly, many of us grew up in families in which the triangle looked quite different.

---

5. I understand that a two-parent family structure does not apply to everyone's situation. However, the dynamics of triangulation are still relevant if you were raised in a different family structure.

WHAT IF YOU ENGAGED YOUR SEXUAL STORY?

For example, I was closer to my mother than my father was. Mom and I had an emotionally closer relationship than Mom had with Dad. Thus, my triangle looked like this:

Figure 7.2

Triangulation Adam

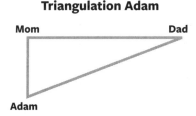

When your triangle looks more like mine, the foundation is set for you to experience significant harm. I am not saying that violation is inevitable; I am saying that the *setup* for violation is present. If the closest emotional bond in your family, for example, is between you and your mother, then your mother often begins looking to you, *as a child*, to meet her adult emotional needs. When this becomes an ongoing pattern, the child has become triangulated.

Triangulation occurs when a parent requires a child to function as an emotional adult by meeting the parent's adult needs and wants.

Here are the critical questions to consider as you ponder the possibility of triangulation in your family:

- Which way did the bulk of the emotional energy flow—from your parent into your heart or from you into your parent's heart?
- Did you *receive more* (emotionally) from your parent, or did your parent *take more* from you emotionally?
- Were you required to give, give, give to your parent, or was your parent continually giving, giving, giving emotionally to you?

Suppose you are a fourteen-year-old girl, and your parents don't have a very close relationship. Your dad begins looking to you, rather than to his wife, for connection. Of course connection between parents and children is a good and healthy thing—unless the parent uses the child to meet their emotional needs, rather than the other way around. Parents and children are not peers. In a healthy parent-child relationship, there is plenty of connection—but the parent never imposes their emotional needs on the child.

The foundation of triangulation is that a parent *takes from* the child rather than *gives to* the child. The root problem is that a parent looks to the child to meet their adult needs. The parent-child relationship is intended to be *nonreciprocal*. In other words, parents are supposed to give, give, give and children are supposed to receive, receive, receive. The parent-child relationship is not designed to be a mutual and balanced relationship as two adults may have.

Perhaps Dad was the parent who always took you to your volleyball and softball games. Just the two of you. And in the car you would sometimes have meaningful conversations. At times, Dad shared how frustrated he was about his relationship with your mother. A child is not supposed to be brought into their parents' marriage.

Or perhaps Dad was always working on his car in the garage. And, for some reason, you often found yourself out in the garage working with him. Spending time with him. Much more frequently than your siblings did. And Mom never did this. It was "special time" between you and your father.

This can appear to be innocent, even sweet and good. After all, what's wrong with a father spending quality time with his daughter? Nothing—as long as Dad is not looking to you to meet his adult emotional needs.

But what if he enjoys your goodness more than he enjoys his wife's goodness? What if your dad actually prefers spending time with you over spending time with his wife? In these cases, it is likely that this "special relationship" is deeply harmful to the child. Significant damage occurs whenever a parent uses a child to satisfy their adult needs.

Looking back, this relationship may feel sweet, but it is actually violating *because the daughter is being used* as a surrogate spouse. The daughter is being *consumed* by her father rather than fathered by him. There is more energy flowing *from* the child *to* the adult rather than vice versa.

IMPORTANT CAVEATS

Many couples go through difficult seasons in which they do not feel emotionally close to one another. This does not mean one parent will necessarily begin triangulating a child. The question is, Are husband and wife emotionally committed to engaging with one another during the difficult season? If not, the critical question then becomes, Does one parent begin to look to a child to satiate their unmet adult emotional needs? Triangulation occurs when parent-child roles get mixed up, and one parent expects a child to meet their needs as if the child were another adult.

If husband and wife don't have a deep emotional connection, and if they are not regularly talking through conflicts and taking responsibility for how they are harming each other, *then the setup exists for one of their children to be triangulated.*

Many people have grown up in single-parent homes. If you grew up with a single parent, does that mean you were necessarily triangulated? By no means. Consider an example of a boy whose parents divorced when he was young, and he was raised primarily by his mother. As long as Mom does not look to her son to meet her emotional needs, then the boy is not being triangulated (even though Dad is absent and the boy has a close emotional connection with Mom).

I know women who are emotionally closer to their children than to their distant husband (or ex-husband). This does not necessarily mean their children are being triangulated. Again, the question is, Does the mother require the child to function as a surrogate spouse in the absence of Dad?

There are also many families in which the dynamics changed over time. Your parents may have divorced. One parent may have died. Your older sister may have been triangulated by your father for much of your life; however, when she left for college, Dad required you to fill that role.

The invitation here is not to categorize yourself as "I was triangulated" or "I was not triangulated." Rather, you are invited to answer the question, In what season of your life did you experience some measure of triangulation, and how might that be affecting your sexuality today?

It's important to remember that you have experienced both intentional and unintentional harm. Triangulation is about a *sustained pattern* of relating between a parent and the chosen child. Relational dynamics are established over years. Isolated incidents may be unintentional, but *patterns* of relating are not.

Moreover, even if you do not believe the harm was intentional, you still have to grapple with its *impact*. The impact of being required to meet a parent's emotional needs is severe. Children are not designed to do that.

THE TWO DEADLY DYNAMICS OF TRIANGULATION

Triangulation results in two deadly dynamics. First, your *goodness is consumed* by one parent. Second, as a result of being consumed by one parent, you are set up to be *envied* by the other parent. Consumed by one parent, envied by the other.[6]

---

6. As with so much in this book, I am indebted to many conversations I've had with Dan Allender, who identified these two dynamics.

Consumption

If your parents weren't each other's best friend—if there was not passionate love and care between them—then you may know something about being consumed and something about being envied. By "being consumed" I mean that since your father knew your mother wasn't there for him, he began to look to you to fill his emotional needs. He began to consume the goodness you brought with your presence.

Triangulation places an immense burden on the chosen child; however, the chosen child rarely *feels* a sense of burden. Quite the opposite! To the child, the relationship will feel loving and sweet and close. As an adult, you will think back on your childhood and remember being highly attuned to the parent who triangulated you—anticipating their needs, reading them well when they were upset, being there for them. You will feel *close* to the parent who made you into a surrogate spouse.

However, "There is nothing loving or caring about a close parent-child relationship when it services the needs and feelings of the parent rather than the child."[7]

If you were triangulated, then the nature of your story is this: **what felt like love wasn't.** This is very hard to come to terms with.

To make matters worse, a triangulated child is not only used by one parent but is also forced into a rivalry with the other parent. What do you think my father thought about the fact that my mother chose me over him? Do you see the setup? I was set up by my mother to be envied by my father. My father (understandably) viewed me as a rival.

Psychologist Kenneth Adams has written a very helpful book on this topic called *Silently Seduced: When Parents Make Their Children Partners*. Dr. Adams shares many examples of people coming to

---

7. Kenneth Adams, *Silently Seduced: When Parents Make Their Children Partners* (Deerfield Beach, FL: Health Communications Inc., 1991), 6.

terms with the triangulation in their family of origin. Here's how one man put it:

> I decided early on I was going to show [my dad] I could be a better father than he ever was. Although I didn't know it at the time, I was also working on being a better husband than he was—*a role my mother always seemed to welcome.*[8]

Notice the dynamic: competition between the son and Dad combined with emotional closeness between the son and Mom.

One of the heart-wrenching realities of children who are triangulated is that it feels *really powerful* to be able to come through for the parent who is treating you like a surrogate spouse. Think of what an ego trip this is for a child! Consider this man's experience:

> It felt so good to be able to make my mom stop crying and put a smile on her face. I was more than willing to be there for her. I felt so important and powerful. *After a while it seemed that my mother actually preferred my company over my father's.*[9]

When this man was a boy, it felt good to be able to comfort his mom. He felt important and powerful . . . he felt *special*.

Lastly, here is an example of a woman looking back on her relationship with her father:

> My father always had me by his side when I was growing up. I was his little sweetie. He and my mother didn't have much of a relationship so I was the *object he adored*. When I was younger, I enjoyed all the attention and closeness.[10]

She "enjoyed" all the attention and closeness. And there *was* goodness in it, but it was also deeply violating because her dad looked

---

8. Adams, *Silently Seduced*, 33. Emphasis mine.
9. Adams, *Silently Seduced*, 52. Emphasis mine.
10. Adams, *Silently Seduced*, 127–28. Emphasis mine.

to her instead of Mom for emotional connection. *She* was the person Dad adored, not Mom. Oh, how that wreaks havoc in a girl's heart—but it's rarely going to feel damaging at the time. This is *subtle*.

If you were triangulated, you likely will not think of yourself as violated or harmed because your relationship with your opposite-sex parent felt *good*—it felt sweet. And it definitely felt better than your relationship with your same-sex parent, who was often critical of you or distant from you.[11] In fact, very often you will live your entire life believing that the parent who triangulated you *was the best parent you had*.

My father was emotionally checked out, and my mother began to look to me for attunement and emotional connection. The best description of my relationship with my mother actually came from my father during a phone call we had when I was forty years old. I began talking to my dad about the emotional closeness between Mom and me. I asked him what he remembered about our relationship and, to my astonishment, this is what he said:

> You and Mom both depended on each other. At the dinner table, you sat across from each other. As the conversation began, you'd look up from your plate and she'd look up from her plate and your eyes would meet. You were looking for a sign—agreement, validation—from one another. Mom was closest to you in terms of brain waves and psychologically. You and Mom always fixed your eyes on one another before anyone else.
>
> Your eyes were always searching for hers and vice versa. Your body language was conjoined, if you know what I mean. You found humor and sadness in the same things; you found agreement about the same things. You were conjoined emotionally. You enjoyed

---

11. Please know that you can also be triangulated by your same-sex parent. For example, I have worked with plenty of women who were required to be their mother's surrogate spouse.

each other's company. You talked to each other with ease. You just seemed connected, very connected.

And I came to envy it. I envied your relationship with your mom. It just seemed pure and honest and mutually helpful. We go through life and we form close associations—I think Mom was your best friend for most of your life. You were very close to her and comfortable with her—it was apparent to everyone. It didn't bother me but I knew I was sort of the odd man out. I wasn't at home much. You spent much more time with Mom.[12]

Dad's words confirmed what my body knew but didn't want to admit: I was triangulated by my mother.

Even if I'd never heard these words from my dad, *my story already contained plenty of data*. **By "data" I mean the particular scenes, vignettes, and anecdotes I partially remembered from my growing-up years. Here is an example of data:**

There is more to my story of calling Mrs. Heidenreich and telling her that I loved her. Later that afternoon—after my heroic phone call—I was in the kitchen with my mom. She had a strange smile on her face as she said to me, "Adam, Mrs. Heidenreich called back and said that she loves you too." I immediately felt a flood of embarrassment fill my six-year-old body. My mom was not supposed to find out about this!

But I didn't *only* feel embarrassment. I also felt something yucky between Mom and me. It was her smile that got me. The particular smile she had on her face let me know she was pleased I had called Mrs. Heidenreich. Why would a mother be pleased that her six-year-old son called a woman across the street and professed his love?

You may be thinking, *Any mom would smile about this story.* But if you had been there—if you had seen the smile—you would have

---

[12]. When I had this phone call, I was sitting at the airport with my headphones in and my computer open. As soon as my dad started talking, I began typing feverishly.

cringed. This was not the endearing smile of a mother enjoying the childlike innocence of her son. This was a mischievous smile. It was the look of a woman who was pleased with her accomplishment. Mom was pleased I had said, "I love you" to Mrs. Heidenreich.

The smile is merely one piece of data. It's insufficient on its own to demonstrate anything. However, when combined with other data points, this piece of data helps reconstruct a crime scene.

One piece of data can be ignored. Two pieces of data can be chalked up to coincidence. But when you have three or more data points, you have to ask yourself, *What truth am I not wanting to see?*

Envy

Consumption is the first deadly dynamic inherent in triangulation; envy is the second. When a child is chosen by one parental figure, the other parental figure comes to envy the chosen child. It is humiliating to know that your spouse prefers someone over you, especially when that someone is a child. As a result, the chosen child frequently bears the contempt and cruelty of the "unchosen" parental figure.

To make matters worse, the chosen child is also forced into a competitive rivalry with any siblings. All children are created for parental delight, and when one is clearly the favorite, the unchosen siblings understandably burn with envy. This, of course, is the Joseph story. The envy-driven hatred of Joseph's brothers was not primarily because Joseph had a pretty coat but because Joseph's father preferred him over all his other children.

Is there tension or distance between you and one of your parents? *Do you know why?* There is always a reason for interpersonal tension or relational distance. There is a reason you have never felt close to your mother. There is a reason your father was often critical or contemptuous of you at the dinner table during holiday gatherings. In order to experience healing—in order for your story to make sense—*you have to identify the reason.*

When I was a sophomore in high school, I struggled with significant levels of anxiety. One day, I found a book at a Christian bookstore called *If God Is So Good, Why Do I Hurt So Bad?* I immediately bought it and began reading it every day. A few days into reading my new book, my dad's brother—my uncle—came to visit. One day my dad and uncle were in the family room, and my uncle saw me reading my book and asked me, "Adam, what are you reading?" I told him the title.

My uncle immediately looked at my father, started laughing scornfully, and said, "I've been asking myself that question my whole life." My father, also laughing, replied with "I know, right." My heart was devastated. I felt humiliated as they joined in contemptuous laughter at my expense. I felt like a loser for thinking that maybe there was a solution to my pain. I was fifteen years old and trying to figure out what it meant to be a man in a painful world . . . and two grown men were laughing at my naivete.

How do you make sense of this story? A surface reading is that my father was simply cruel. However, human beings are intentional creatures. There is always a reason for our cruelty. Why was my father so committed to humiliating me? Because he was not fond of the fact that his wife preferred me—an adolescent—to him, a grown man. My father was (understandably) envious that his wife chose to emotionally connect more with me than with him.

The story of my strained relationship with my dad doesn't make sense until it is understood through the lens of the triangulation with my mom.

When you have been triangulated, it can be very hard to name it. When you are required to function like a surrogate spouse to one of your parents, your childhood is stolen. This is because *you can't fully be a kid when you are often required to be an adult.* You can't be a carefree child when you are preoccupied by a parent's emotional well-being.

WHEN TRIANGULATION IS SEXUALIZED

When triangulation is present in a family, it is common (though not inevitable) for the triangulated relationship to become sexualized. By "sexualized," I mean that there is erotic energy between the parent and the chosen child.

There are intimate relational dynamics at play in families that we don't tend to think of as erotic, but they are. Eroticism is not merely a matter of genital contact. It is far more about the eyes than about the hands. It is more about *the energy between two people* than about what is happening with body parts. Eroticism pertains to what makes the body come alive.

Here are some signs a parent-child relationship was sexualized:

- When you hugged Mom/Dad, the hugs lasted slightly longer than was comfortable and/or the hugs felt a little "gross" or "weird."
- Mom/Dad made sexually suggestive comments about your body or appearance.
- You felt uncomfortable wearing attractive clothes in front of Mom/Dad.
- Something felt a little off when you danced with Mom/Dad at your wedding.

Triangulation that becomes sexualized is properly called subtle sexual abuse. It's subtle in that there may not have been *any* inappropriate physical touch. It's sexual in that the energy between the adult and the child is erotically charged.

Can you be subtly sexually abused if you were never inappropriately touched by someone? Absolutely. Again, sexuality is far more about the eyes than the hands and genitals. Most women know what it's like to be gazed upon by lustful eyes that are attempting to sexualize the interaction. The man could be halfway across the room—zero physical touch—and yet it is a sexually violating interaction. I couldn't have named it when I was a boy, but at times there was sexual energy when my mom looked at me and interacted with me.

Please understand that subtle does not equate to "less severe." In my counseling practice, I have found this phenomenon of subtle sexual abuse to be the root of immense torment for many people and the root of many problems with sexuality in adulthood. Triangulation can be particularly painful because it flies under the radar and, once reckoned with, unravels long-held perceptions of our parents and ourselves.

WHAT IF YOU WEREN'T TRIANGULATED?

You may not have been the triangulated child in your family. If you had siblings, that burden may have fallen to a brother or sister. However, the fallout from their triangulation will still affect you. Consider the following two sisters, Cheryl and Susan.

> Mom and Dad did not have a healthy marriage built on love, companionship, and frequent repair of ruptures. Instead, Mom and Dad grew increasingly distant from each other and increasingly contemptuous of one another.
>
> As a result, Cheryl's father began to look to Cheryl for emotional support and companionship. He would go to all her field hockey games and, although Mom came to some of the games, it was clear that there was a bond between Cheryl and Dad that was closer than the bond between Mom and Dad. Cheryl was the triangulated child—the chosen child.
>
> Susan was the *unchosen younger sister*.
>
> Susan was spared the madness of being triangulated by her father; however, she wore the crown of "unchosen." Susan always had a vague sense that Dad preferred her older sister, Cheryl, and this awareness was devastating. Moreover, throughout her

growing-up years, Susan felt a nagging sense of envy and resentment toward Cheryl . . . and *never knew exactly why*. Susan actually liked Cheryl, but sometimes her envy and resentment would manifest in cruelty toward her. Susan was left feeling unchosen by her father and ashamed of her cruelty toward her sister. The only "good thing" in Susan's life was that Mom was nicer to Susan than she was to Cheryl.

It is hard to overstate the heartache that comes with being unchosen. Imagine being twelve-year-old Susan. What happens inside your body when you watch Dad light up when he talks about your older sister but not when he talks about you? It is a deep agony to hear the warmth in Dad's tone of voice for her but not for you.

Moreover, you also bear the heartache of envying your sister. Because of the triangulation, you are robbed of a pure and sweet relationship with your sibling. It is polluted because of Dad's favoritism.

I worked with a woman who experienced a very different tucking-in ritual than her older sister. Dad was the one who put both sisters to bed each night. However, after Dad tucked in my client, he would go into the kitchen, slice a red apple, and carry the slices on a cutting board to my client's older sister's room. My client then had to listen as her dad and her older sister talked about their day and ate the apple slices together. This happened every night for years.

If you are the unchosen sibling, you carry debris in your body because of the triangulation. For example, how might Susan's "unchosenness" affect her sexuality as she grows up? One of the most common potential consequences is that she will begin to do anything to be chosen by a man since she wasn't chosen by her father—including using her sexuality.

You may have been the Cheryl in your family, or you may have been the Susan. Either way, there is fallout for *all of the children* when one is triangulated.

HOW SEXUAL "CHOICES" MAY BE ROOTED IN YOUR PAST STORY

Sexual choices are far more complex, nuanced, and complicated than most people want to acknowledge, especially most Christians.

Choice is not the same for all people. The brain of a securely attached person is very different from the brain of an insecurely attached person. And it is your brain that makes your choices.

Consider two men, Isaiah and Michael.

Isaiah grew up in a home in which his Big Six needs were met. His parents were attuned, responsive, and engaged with him. Isaiah's affect was sufficiently regulated by his parents, and his fear, sadness, and anger were welcomed in his home. When his parents harmed him, they apologized and sought to make it right.

Michael, by contrast, grew up in a very different home. His mother was intimidating and contemptuous. She would often mock Michael at the dinner table. Michael's dad was emotionally withdrawn and rarely advocated for him.

Neither parent was attuned, responsive, or engaged with Michael. As a result, his body was often flooded with anxiety. One day, he discovered masturbation. Finally, he could do something to soothe his anxiety and help reduce his body's high levels of cortisol. Masturbation was the only means he found available to him for soothing because his parents were unwilling to provide any soothing, care, or containment for his pain.

Today, Isaiah and Michael are thirty-five-year-old men with very different brains. The choice to go home after work and look at pornography is very different for Isaiah and Michael.

Michael is going to have a much harder time choosing not to look at pornography than Isaiah.

Because Michael's brain is very different from Isaiah's brain.

Michael learned to cope with his emotional pain by soothing himself through masturbation. As a result, Michael's brain has been *primed* to masturbate when he is in emotional pain. Again, priming refers to the likelihood that particular neural networks will fire in the present *based on past experience*. Priming is why choice is not the same for all people.

Priming means that Michael's brain will be more inclined to self-soothe with masturbation because of his past story.

And look: *God knows this.* God knows how your brain has been primed.

I am not excusing Michael. What I'm saying is that the "choice" to go home after a hard day at work and look at pornography is not the same for all people.

If the church is going to recover its relevance for real life, we need a far more robust understanding of sin. The question is not, Is Michael choosing to sin? The question is, *Why* is Michael choosing to look at pornography?

Michael's repentance needs to be far deeper than "I repent of looking at pornography tonight." It will require him to engage the particular ways in which he was wounded. This is a much more robust understanding of repentance.[13]

HOW LOW SEXUAL DESIRE MAY BE ROOTED IN YOUR PAST STORY

For many of us, the sexual struggle is not about inordinate desire but about little to no sexual desire at all. Sexual abuse in any form, subtle or overt, affects the part of our brain that desires. Moreover, developmental trauma—that is, not getting your Big Six needs met

---

13. For more on how your past story is linked to your present sexual behavior, see Jay Stringer's book *Unwanted*.

as a child—also profoundly affects the part of our brain that desires, that has longing. As a result, many of us have difficulty with our Wanter.

What is your relationship to your desires? I don't merely mean sexual desire, though I'm including that. How do you feel about your longings, your desires? It is very common to be deeply ambivalent about them.

There are two primary reasons for our complicated relationship to our desires. First, for anyone with a history of sexual harm, desiring something—wanting something—can *feel dangerous*. This is because our brains believe our desires are what got us abused in the first place. Abusers gain access to victims through *grooming*, which is the process whereby an abuser meets some of the unmet longings in their victim's heart—such as the longing to be seen, to be noticed, to be paid attention to, to be cared about.

Most abusers are very skilled at meeting some of our Big Six needs. They give a taste of attunement, responsiveness, and engagement. And since we were created to need these things, *something in our hearts comes alive*. And we desire more. And it is in that context that we are sexually harmed by our abusers.

Therefore, if you have been abused, your brain has paired your desire for care, for connection, for being seen and noticed with "Something bad is about to happen to me." As a result, you now feel a sense of danger well up inside whenever you allow yourself to desire, to long for something. Remember, neurons that fire together, wire together. When you are sexually abused, your neurons for "This attention and care feel really good" fire at the same time as the neurons for "This sexual violation feels terrifying and awful." Those two neural networks become paired with each other. Whenever your neurons fire for "This attention and care feel really good," your brain will also fire the neurons associated with the terror and violation of sexual abuse. As a result, your brain may have learned that the part of you that "wants" is dangerous. As far as your brain is concerned, *If I hadn't wanted their care and attention, I wouldn't have been sexually harmed.*

The second reason many of us are ambivalent about our desires is because if we are insecurely attached, we have a truckload of unmet desires in the basement of our hearts. And we've been carrying around these unmet longings for years and years. Avoidantly attached individuals often deal with these unmet desires for relational connection by shutting down the attachment circuitry in their brain—that is, by shutting down the parts of their brain *that want, that long, that yearn.* And this sometimes includes the part of them that wants sexually, the part of them that desires sexual things. Their sexual Wanter is shut down.

If you let yourself connect with your sexual desires, you risk *reactivating* that part of your brain that has been so deeply wounded—that part of your brain that holds a storehouse of unmet desires. This is a deeply disappointed part of you. It is a desperate part of you. You don't want to get connected to your unmet longing. And so you shut down your Wanter.

To say it another way, you don't *let yourself* have sexual desire for your partner. In marriage counseling, you'll say things like "I just don't have as much sexual desire as my partner." And sometimes this is true. However, oftentimes it would be more true to say, "I'm terrified of letting myself feel my sexual desire for my partner, and so I shut down any desire before it develops." In other words, *"I don't want to want."*

For some of us, wanting makes us nervous. Wanting makes us anxious. Wanting makes us feel way too vulnerable.

You may (understandably) find comfort and safety in knowing your partner wants you more than you want them. You find emotional safety in knowing your partner has more sexual desire for you than you have for them. It gives you a sense of control in the relationship, which you never had as a child.

Please don't hear this as an accusation. *There is a reason* you have shut down your Wanter. A good reason.

CHAPTER 7 KEY POINTS

- There is a linkage between your present sexual struggles and your past sexual story, particularly in your family of origin.
- Sexual harm in the past becomes reenacted in the present. This is because you have neurons, and that's how neurons operate.
- No one makes it to adulthood without experiencing some form of sexual harm.
- The primary way evil assaults your sexuality is through the introduction of sexual shame.
- Sexual abuse comes in two forms: sexual contact and sexual interactions. Both are severely damaging.
- The primary damage from sexual abuse can best be described in one word: *complicity*.
- Triangulation occurs when a parent requires a child to function as an emotional adult by meeting the parent's adult needs and wants.
- Triangulation often becomes sexualized.

TRIANGULATION EXERCISE

In the space below, draw your triangle. Remember, the closeness of the points of the triangle represents the closeness of the relationships between you, your mother, and your father. (Note: you may have to draw multiple triangles to account for situations of divorce and remarriage or parental death and remarriage. Alternatively, you may have been raised by a single parent; in this case, try to depict the emotional closeness of your relationship with your single parent.)

The questions that follow are designed to help you think about the relational triangles in your family of origin.

Mom and Dad's Marital Relationship

Rate the items below on a scale of 1 to 5.

1=Never, 2=Rarely, 3=Occasionally, 4=Usually, 5=Always

_____ Mom and Dad were close friends.

_____ Mom and Dad enjoyed each other and spent time doing things just the two of them.

_____ Mom and Dad were attuned to each other.

_____ Mom and Dad were honest with each other about their feelings.

_____ Mom and Dad showed physical affection for one another (hugging, hand-holding, cuddling).

_____ When Mom was mad/sad/afraid, Dad responded to her with comfort and care.

_____ When Dad was mad/sad/afraid, Mom responded to him with comfort and care.

_____ When Mom and Dad disagreed or experienced conflict, they talked things through and reconnected with each other.

Based on your responses above, how close would you say your parents were to each other?

_____

_____

_____

Your Relationship with Mom and Dad

_____ Mom talked to me about her marriage problems.

_____ Dad talked to me about his marriage problems.

_____ Mom and I were emotionally closer than she was with Dad.

_____ Dad and I were emotionally closer than he was with Mom.

_____ I was Mom's favorite.

_____ I was Dad's favorite.

_____ Mom made sexually suggestive comments (sexual jokes or comments about my or others' appearance, weight, or body parts).

_____ Dad made sexually suggestive comments (sexual jokes or comments about my or others' appearance, weight, or body parts).

_____ Mom confided in me about her emotional problems and difficulties. I felt like her confidant. We had a special relationship.

_____ Dad confided in me about his emotional problems and difficulties. I felt like his confidant. We had a special relationship.

_____ One of my parents attended most of my special events (games, concerts, recitals) while the other parent stayed home.

Based on your responses, would you say that you were required as a child/adolescent to meet some of the adult needs of your father or mother?

8

WHAT IF YOU LISTENED TO THE STORY YOUR BODY IS TELLING YOU?

> Mr. Duffy lived a short distance from his body.
> James Joyce, *Dubliners*

> And everything that has happened to you has happened to your bodies. Every act of violence, every moment of pleasure . . . every kindness, every sorrow. Every ounce of laughter. We carry all of it with us in some form or another. We are walking embodiments of our entire story.
> Nadia Bolz Weber, "Resurrection Is Messy"

The body speaks. *Your body* speaks. It has spoken in the past, and it is speaking now. One way your body speaks is through your physical sensations. Your body communicates with you via shifts in sensation. Do you listen to it? Do you listen to the voice of your cells, tissues, organs, and muscles?

As you go about your day, your body experiences different physical sensations. All the time. There are times you may not be *aware* that your body is experiencing particular sensations, but it is.

Always.

There are other times when you are likely *very* aware that your body is experiencing a particular sensation. For example, if you are afraid of snakes and you see one, your heart will begin to race, your chest will tighten, and you may experience a trembling in your stomach. We call this combination of sensations "fear." It's important to understand that although fear is an emotion, it is *first* a particular combination of bodily sensations. In fact, every emotion is a combination of bodily sensations.

Examples of bodily sensations include tightness in the jaw, clenched teeth, a racing heart, trembling in the chest, a knot in the back, butterflies in the stomach, or a lump in the throat. Some people experience anger as a tightness in the jaw combined with a more rapid heartbeat. Others experience anger as clenched teeth and a tightening of the fist.

Throughout your day, the various regions of your body (head, throat, shoulders, chest, arms, gut, pelvis, legs) feel lesser or greater degrees of tightness, constriction, heaviness, warmth, and so forth. These sensations tell the truth about your present experience.

In other words, your body is a truth-teller.

It is *the trustworthy prophet from within.*

A prophetic truth-teller that is always with you.

What a gift! You may not know what truth your bodily sensations are telling, but your body doesn't lie. It can't.

This does not mean your body always perceives reality accurately. By no means. If you have a history of trauma, you will likely feel fear at times when there is actually no real danger. Is your body lying to you then? Deceiving you? No. In these instances your body is telling you the truth *about your story* rather than telling you the truth about the present situation.

Your body is always revealing *some* truth to you—even if you don't know what that truth is in the moment.

It can be difficult to listen to your body when you lack a vocabulary for the wide variety of sensations in your body. This lack makes it very difficult to notice subtle shifts in sensation. In the spirit of building a vocabulary, here is a list of bodily sensations.

achy	electric	open
alive	empty	prickly
bloated	energized	pulsing
blocked	faint	quivering
breathless	fluttery	radiating
brittle	frantic	shuddering
burning	frozen	spacious
buzzing	fuzzy	suffocating
clammy	heavy	tender
closed	hot	tense
cold	icy	throbbing
congested	jittery	tight
constricted	jumpy	tingly
contracted	knotted	trembling
cramped	light	vibrating
dense	limp	warm
dizzy	nauseous	wobbly
dull	numb	

Over the past couple of years, my jaw has often been clenched and tight. Whenever I scan my body, the place where I most notice tension is in my jaw (and cheeks). I have been paying more attention to this tension. As I spend time noticing this very unpleasant sensation, I've begun to ask it, *What do you want me to know?*

It may come as a surprise, but the sensations in your body *will answer questions* if you take the time to listen. If you take your bodily sensations seriously, they will speak to you. In my case, the tension in my jaw responded by saying, *You never pay attention to me.* In other words, there is a part of me I am neglecting and ignoring. A part of me that likely needs curiosity and care.

Whenever I am engaging a client's story, one of the most helpful questions I ask is, "What are you feeling in your body right now?" I ask my client to scan their body and notice any sensations they are currently experiencing. Sometimes a client will respond with, "I feel a tightness in my chest, like a heaviness pressing down."

I always reply, "Notice that."

These are two of the most important words in therapy.

Notice that.

Without a doubt, these two words bear more fruit in the therapeutic process than any other two words. Why? Because they are an invitation to listen to the story your body is trying to tell you!

Anytime you are exploring your story—whether it's in a group setting or one-on-one with a counselor—the smartest entity in the room is *your physical body*. Not your brain. Not the counselor's brain. *Your* physical body.

For my clients with tightness in their chests, that tightness is their body's way of communicating very important information. The way they listen to that communication is by taking a minute to attune to the sensations in their chest and simply notice what it's like to really *feel* that tightness and that "heaviness pressing down."

I give them a minute or two to feel the feeling in their chest, to really take it in and notice it. If they pay attention to the feeling with a posture of kindness and curiosity, the sensation will reveal more truth. In other words, the sensation will speak.

My next question is, "If that tight feeling in your chest could talk, what would it say?"

Oh, the riches of the wisdom that pours forth in response to this question!

As you let the sensations in your body speak, they will lead you further into uncovering the truth of your story. If that sensation could talk, what would it say? Here are some of the answers my clients have shared with me:

"It would say, 'Stop silencing me, Mom.'"

"It would say, 'I can't bear this any longer.'"

"It would say, 'I can't breathe.'"

"It wouldn't say any words, it would just scream . . . for hours."

Awareness of her bodily sensations led my client Tiffany to new levels of freedom in her relationship with her mother.

> Tiffany's relationship with her mother was a source of constant tension, heartache, and struggle. Whenever Tiffany would risk expressing disappointment in her mom, Mom would respond by blaming Tiffany for something. For example, as a junior in high school, Tiffany wanted to buy a new dress for prom but her mother wouldn't let her. When Tiffany pleaded, Mom snapped back, "You're the most ungrateful girl in your school."
>
> This became a pattern: when Tiffany would express longing or disappointment, she would be met with blame and accusation. The purpose of the blame and accusation was to silence Tiffany. And it worked! As Tiffany felt the shame of being ungrateful, she would lose her words and eventually leave the conversation. Once I named this pattern, Tiffany remembered another story with her

mom from when she was in first grade. Mom had planned a birthday party for Tiffany, but only two of the five invited kids could come on the scheduled date. Tiffany said to her mom, "I don't want to have the party this Saturday. I want to do it next Saturday, when everyone can come."

Tiffany's mom became quite angry and said, "What's wrong with you, Tiffany? Don't you like the two friends who are coming? Don't you know how hard I worked to plan your party for this coming Saturday? Stop being so self-centered." Notice the pattern: Tiffany expresses disappointment, and Mom blames and accuses Tiffany of being bad in some way.

After she shared this story with me, I asked Tiffany to check in with her body and see what sensations she was experiencing. She noticed a constriction in her throat. I invited her to take a minute and feel it. After a minute, I said, "If that feeling in your throat could talk, what would it say?" Tiffany replied, "It wouldn't say anything; it would just scream." I asked her, "What would it scream?"

"It would scream, 'Stop blaming me for everything! Just shut up and stop blaming me anytime I tell you I'm disappointed about something!'"

Tiffany could have talked with me for hours without getting where she got in ten minutes by listening to her body and letting her body lead the exploration.

In summary, here is the sequence of inquiry:

1. What are you feeling in your body right now?
2. Notice that.
3. If that sensation in your chest/gut/throat/shoulders/back/arms/legs could talk, what would it say?

This line of curiosity almost always bears fruit—which is to say, you become aware of important truths your body wants you to know.

It's important to understand that your body knows things that your enskulled brain does not. I say "enskulled brain" because you actually have three brains—there are brain cells in your heart, brain cells in your gut, and brain cells in your brain. You have likely heard phrases such as "Listen to your heart" or "Trust your gut." These phrases recognize that your heart and your gut are *places of knowing*, just like your enskulled brain is also a place of knowing.

Dan Siegel says, "Our heart and gut offer insight, intuition, and even wisdom that the third brain, the enskulled brain, can act on."[1] The point is that your heart and your gut have brain cells that know things.

Your "Knower" is what I call the brain cells in your gut and heart—brain cells that have lots of knowledge and continually offer you trustworthy information.

What if you began to listen to your Knower?

This may be a better question: What makes you reluctant to listen to your Knower?

Your body from the neck down knows things *about your story* that your enskulled brain does not know. Like a trusted compass, it can guide you into the truth of your story. Your body is constantly trying to reveal the truth of your story to you.

However, before continuing our exploration of the body's wisdom, we need to overcome a hurdle that keeps many people from listening to their body.

CAN YOU TRUST YOUR BODY?

Many modern Western churches are infected with a deep suspicion of the physical body. The body is often viewed as secondary to the

---

1. Daniel Siegel, *IntraConnected: Mwe (Me + We) as the Integration of Self, Identity, and Belonging*, Norton Series on Interpersonal Neurobiology (New York: W. W. Norton, 2023), 105.

soul. In other words, the soul is the part of you that really matters, and your physical body is merely a vehicle for it.

If you grew up in one of these churches, you have likely received the message that your gut/heart/body is untrustworthy. It's the idea that *you should not let your feelings guide you*. Someone recently said to me, "If I allowed myself to follow my heart, my life would be a mess right now."

When I was growing up, there was a very popular sermon illustration designed to hammer home the idea that feelings were not to be trusted. It was an illustration of a train. The engine of the train was labeled "FACTS," the second car was labeled "FAITH," and the caboose was labeled "FEELINGS." The point of the illustration was that you couldn't rely on your feelings. Indeed, if you wanted your life to go well, you needed to put your faith in the facts of Scripture rather than letting your feelings guide you.

Each time I heard this illustration, I walked away thinking to myself, *Adam, you can't trust your feelings*. My feelings were only valid if they lined up with the facts of the Bible. I came to believe that my feelings were not a reliable guide, and I should not make decisions based on them. This illustration was just one example of my church's teaching that it was dangerous to rely on *the wisdom of one's body*.

Various Bible verses are often used to support the claim that we should not trust the body—and by "body" here I mean our gut feelings, intuition, and heart sense. For example, Proverbs 3:5 says, "Trust in the Lord with all your heart and lean not on your own understanding." This verse is often quoted to convince people not to trust their Knower. For me, "lean not on your own understanding" came to mean that a real Christian does not trust themself. A real Christian ignores their intuition when it conflicts with what the Bible seems to say. A good Christian denies their own understanding of reality when the Bible seems to say something different.

This kind of teaching has profoundly shaped evangelicalism. As a result, if you grew up in this kind of Christian culture, you may (understandably) distrust your intuition, emotions, and gut sense—your Knower. In other words, you may believe that *external* authority is a more trustworthy guide than *internal* authority.

However, having an inner Knower is *part of being created in the image of God*. Internal authority is about trusting the part of you that is capable of knowing and discerning rightly. In contrast, external authority refers to trusting the wisdom of others (wisdom that comes from outside of your body).

I am not suggesting you discount the wisdom of others. Nor am I suggesting that you rely *only* on your feelings and intuition. However, your feelings are always (a) honest, (b) telling you some truth about either the present or the past, and (c) worth listening to and being curious about.

If you grew up in the evangelical church, there is no way you escaped the message that *external authority is to be trusted over internal authority*. This is a spiritually abusive teaching but a popular one nonetheless.

Here's my point: before you can listen to the truths your body is trying to tell you, *you may need to restore trust in your body.*

You may need to come home again to your inner Knower and learn to trust it anew.

It's hard to overstate the importance of coming home to your own precious body.

Last year I was scrolling through Instagram and noticed someone had asked their followers to share in the comments section "Any Bible verses that have been used against you." Scores of people responded, and the most frequently mentioned verse was Jeremiah 17:9, which says, "The heart is deceitful above all things and beyond cure. Who can understand it?"

Here is a sampling of the kinds of comments people made about how this verse had been used against them:

> "This verse was used to reinforce the idea that whatever I wanted was bad. If my heart is deceitful above all things, I can't trust myself."

> "Jeremiah 17:9 taught me that my desires couldn't be trusted and to never look within myself for answers."

> "When I felt God calling me to become a musician, my parents used Jeremiah 17:9 to convince me I was wrong. They argued that I might feel like God was calling me to be a musician, but since my heart was deceitful above all things, I shouldn't act on that feeling."

> "Because of Jeremiah 17:9, I have absolutely no trust in my own feelings or intuition. I feel like my heart is evil and untrustworthy."

> "How am I supposed to make decisions if my heart is deceitful above all things?"

What is going on here? Jeremiah 17:9 is often used to cause people

to distrust *their own feelings*,

to disbelieve their own *thoughts*, and

to question their own *gut*.

Here's the tragic irony: one of the primary points of the book of Jeremiah is that your heart is actually trustworthy.

In Jeremiah 31, we read the following:

> "The days are coming," declares the Lord,
>   "when I will make a new covenant
> with the people of Israel
>   and with the people of Judah. . . .

> I will put my law in their minds
> and write it on their hearts." (vv. 31, 33)

God promises to write his law *on your heart*. Yes, that same heart that is supposed to be deceitful above all things. This promise of God is fulfilled in Jesus Christ and the sending of the Holy Spirit. The point of Jeremiah 31 is that your heart is *good*.

You can't possibly read the whole book of Jeremiah and think to yourself, *Jeremiah believes that his heart is deceitful above all things and beyond cure*. Quite to the contrary. Jeremiah believes deeply in the goodness and rightness of his own heart.

Consider this text from Jeremiah 12. The prophet is talking to God, and he says:

> Why does the way of the wicked prosper? . . .
> You are always on their lips
> but far from their hearts.
> Yet you know me, LORD;
> you see me and test my thoughts about you. (vv. 1–3)

Jeremiah's entire argument here is that his heart is not deceitful above all things . . . on the contrary, his heart is good, and the hearts of the wicked are deceitful.

It's not just Jeremiah who insists that his heart is good. The psalmists do it also. A lot.

> Vindicate me, LORD, according to my righteousness,
> according to my integrity, O Most High. (Ps. 7:8)

> The LORD has dealt with me according to my righteousness;
> according to the cleanness of my hands he has
> rewarded me. (18:20)

> Vindicate me, LORD,
> for I have led a blameless life;

> I have trusted in the Lord
> and have not faltered. (26:1)

And then there's the book of Job. The starting point of Job—the foundation upon which the entire narrative rests—is God's claim (yes, God's claim) that Job's heart is righteous and good. Here's how God puts it in Job 2:

> Then the Lord said to Satan, "Have you considered my servant Job? There is no one on earth like him; he is blameless and upright, a man who fears God and shuns evil." (v. 3)

Blameless and upright! *God* says Job's heart is good.

It's important to understand that none of these verses are claims of perfection. When a psalmist or Job says, "I am blameless," they are not talking about sinlessness. No one is saying, "I am without sin." (The notion of sinlessness did not exist in the Hebrew imagination.) They are saying, "My heart is good and trustworthy even though I do, of course, sin."

The point I'm keen to make is that none of these biblical writers believed their heart was deceitful above all things and beyond cure.

When a Bible verse is used to convince you not to trust yourself, this enters the realm of spiritual abuse.

Moreover, one of the central themes of the New Testament is that our bodies have become the dwelling place of God. This is one of the apostle Paul's most significant theological claims, succinctly summarized in 1 Corinthians 6:19:

> Do you not know that your bodies are temples of the Holy Spirit, who is in you, whom you have received from God?

To understand the full meaning of Paul's claim, it's important to remember that in ancient Israel, the temple was the place where heaven and earth intersected. In other words, in the Old Testament,

God dwelled in the temple. In light of this, it is astonishing for Paul to claim that the human body has become a temple. Paul is saying that the glory of God, which previously resided in the Jerusalem temple, can now reside in the human body.[2]

AFFECT DYSREGULATION

The primary way your body speaks to you is through your affect. (For a reminder about what affect is, see chapter 4.) Following is a graphic that depicts the affect spectrum:

Figure 8.1

AFFECT REGULATION

1 2 3 4 5 6 7 8 9 10

Hypoarousal	Regulated	Hyperarousal
Emotions: shame, hopelessness and/or despair	Emotions: relaxed excitement	Emotions: panic, terror, and/or rage
Sensations: numbness/ shutdown, shallow breathing, difficulty concentrating, sleepiness	Sensations: calm, alert, attentive	Sensations: racing heart, faster breathing, tightening in the chest or stomach, jitteriness
	(the sweet zone of 4-7)	

Copyright 2017 Adam Young

You may be wondering, Why is it so important to know when my body becomes dysregulated? Answer: because whenever you become dysregulated, your nervous system is letting you know valuable information about your present environment and about your past story.

Dysregulation makes implicit memory known.

In other words, when your body becomes dysregulated, there is a reason for that! Every single time. And that reason is rooted in either your present circumstances or your story (or, most likely, both).

---

2. See also Ephesians 2:19–22 and 1 Corinthians 3:16.

Indeed, when it comes to your "body story," the most important category to pay attention to is your affect. The shift into various levels of dysregulation during your day is the primary way your body reveals your story to you. Therefore, by noticing when you become dysregulated, you can learn important things about your story.

What kinds of things dysregulate you? A child having a meltdown? Your partner looking at their phone as you are trying to talk with them? Making a mistake at work? It's important to become aware of the kinds of things that send your nervous system into a dysregulated state.

Once you become aware you are dysregulated, the next step is to name whether you are hyperaroused or hypoaroused. Because, again, your nervous system's tendency to either amp up or shut down is *enstoried*. It's not genetic and it's not random. There is a reason for this, and the reason is rooted in your stories.

Generally speaking, ambivalently attached people tend toward hyperarousal, and avoidantly attached people tend toward hypoarousal. It is also common to amp up to hyperarousal (panic, terror, and/or rage) as you desperately try to get another person to respond to you, and, if/when that doesn't work, slam down to hypoarousal (hopelessness, shame, and/or despair). The invitation is to pay close attention to the tendencies of your particular nervous system.

The third and final step is to bring some curiosity to your dysregulated body by asking yourself the question, *What might have caused me to get dysregulated just now?*

In summary, here are the three steps to listening to the story your affect is telling you:

1. Notice when you get dysregulated.
2. Identify whether you are hypoaroused or hyperaroused.

3. Be curious about what present circumstance/experience/event prompted the dysregulation, and what your dysregulation is revealing about your past story.

Here is an example of how dysregulation in the present is linked to the past.

Lawrence has a seven-year-old son, Patrick, who cries often. Lawrence, however, was never allowed to cry as a child. Whenever Patrick's crying lasts longer than Lawrence thinks is appropriate, something inside Lawrence's body begins to change. As the crying continues, Lawrence's body becomes dysregulated. Amped up with both panic and anger, Lawrence enters a state of hyperarousal (8–10 range).

Now, the question is, Why does Patrick's crying catalyze Lawrence's body to become dysregulated?

Lawrence's wife doesn't get dysregulated when Patrick cries. And, of equal importance, Lawrence doesn't get dysregulated when his daughter cries. Only his son. So, what's going on?

As soon as Patrick cries for more than a few minutes, something inside Lawrence screams, *I held it together as a kid. I never did what Patrick does on a weekly basis. Why can't my son hold it together like I always had to?* In short, Lawrence's body is becoming dysregulated because his son is allowed to do what Lawrence was never allowed to do as a boy. And Lawrence has not yet addressed that heartache from his past story.

Until Lawrence addresses his family of origin story—particularly the fact that he was never allowed to cry—he is not going to be able to tolerate Patrick's crying. It's not the crying per se that is triggering Lawrence (remember, he doesn't dysregulate when his daughter cries); it is that the crying reminds him he was not allowed to cry when he was Patrick's age.

The word *trigger* is very common today. But what does it mean? A *trigger* is any event in the outside world that catalyzes your body to enter a physiological state of stress. A trigger is anything that dysregulates your affect.

Now, the question is, Why does situation x trigger you? Answer: Because you are remembering something. Is *remembering* the correct verb? Yes. Your brain is calling something to mind from your past. However, since the situation is activating implicit memory rather than explicit memory, you don't have the sensation of recall (see chapter 6). You don't know you are remembering something. That's what a trigger is.

IMPULSES: WHAT MOVEMENTS DOES YOUR BODY WANT TO MAKE?

In addition to shifts in bodily sensations and shifts in affect, your body also experiences impulses to movement. Regularly, throughout your day. An *impulse* is an inclination or desire to move your body in a particular way. For example, if you are at the grocery store and see someone you don't like, you might feel a bodily impulse to turn your cart around and go in a different direction. Conversely, if you see someone you are quite fond of, you might feel a bodily impulse to extend your arms and offer a hug.

If you have a history of trauma, it is likely that:

> You were taught from an early age to resist your bodily impulses.
>
> You are often unaware of your bodily impulses today.
>
> You frequently ignore or dismiss your body's inclinations to move in a particular way (when you are aware of them).

One way to become more connected to your body's inclinations to movement is by using your imagination. Think about visiting your parents' house for Thanksgiving or Christmas or going to some other family gathering. As you imagine sitting at the dinner table or in the family room, what does your body *want* to do?

You may have the bodily impulse to stay there forever because it's such a deeply joyful experience. In contrast, you may have the bodily impulse to throw a plate across the room just to stop the socially nice but devastatingly boring conversation that always dominates family gatherings. You may have the impulse to push your chair five feet back from the table because you don't want to be associated with these people. You may feel the impulse to throw your glass of water in your stepfather's face because you're sick and tired of his misogynistic jokes. You may have the bodily impulse to shrink yourself down to one-tenth your size so that no one notices you and no one talks to you. The scenarios are endless, but you get the point. If you allow yourself to settle into your body as you activate your imagination, you will discover you have lots of bodily impulses inside.

Please hear me well: I'm not suggesting you act on all of your bodily impulses. I'm suggesting that you *pay attention* to them and let them teach you about your story and your nervous system.

Because your bodily impulses are *enstoried*.

In other words, the inclination to move your body in a particular way is not random. All bodily impulses are a product of your past experiences in life.

For example, I have worked with many women who have a bodily impulse to make themselves physically smaller when they go out in public. Their shoulders curve inward and downward in an attempt to make their breasts less noticeable. These women have a history of sexual abuse, and their bodies have responded to their experiences by developing the impulse to hide anything that might make them more likely to be abused again in the future.

Over time, bodily impulses cause changes in body posture. If you look at the way people hold themselves, you will learn something about their story.

Try this experiment, first in private and then in public. It is simple: pull your shoulders back and push your chest out a little bit... and then notice what you feel inside. Notice how your feelings shift as you intentionally adjust the appearance of your physical body.

Here's another experiment. Notice what you feel inside when you extend your hand and arm out in front of you, as you reach. The reach can feel very vulnerable to people with a history of not having their needs met. What does it feel like for you to extend your arm out, open your hand, and reach for help?

A man came to see me because of "relationship problems." It became clear that he lived a lonely and isolated life. I invited this man to reach out his hand and make a beckoning motion, which is a reach followed by a grasp and a pull. As he used his arm and hand to make that motion, he said, "This feels very uncomfortable to me. I never reach for help from someone else."

In summary, your story is written in the cells, tissues, and musculature of your physical body. The way you hold your shoulders back or slightly hunched forward speaks volumes about your past experiences in life.

YOUR POSTURE TOWARD YOUR BODY

Before concluding this chapter, it may prove very helpful to consider your posture toward your body. In other words, How do you feel about your body? Let me move closer: How do you feel about your thighs? Your nose? Your breasts? Your stomach area? What part of your body are you the most fond of? The least fond of?

Whatever your answer, there is a reason for that. And that reason is rooted in your story. Said another way, if you tell me you've hated your thighs since high school, you are telling me precious information about your story. You didn't come out of the womb hating your thighs.

Most of us have experienced the cursing of one or more parts of our bodies. Cursing happens when someone in a position of authority or influence names a part of your body as less than lovely. Cursing can be subtle or not so subtle:

> "When you're older and a boy tries to kiss you, he's going to run into your nose."
>
> "You'll never be able to get a brush through that hair."
>
> "If you keep eating like that, your thighs won't fit in this house."

Notice what you feel in your body as you read these sentences. Each of them is a curse. Curses take up residence inside of you. As a ten-year-old, you can't say to yourself, *Mom is being incredibly cruel right now and cursing my thighs. I'm not going to let her words mark me. I don't agree with Mom's curse. In fact, I bless the goodness of my thighs.* A ten-year-old can't do that. The dilemma is that if curses are not renounced and replaced with blessing, the only alternative is to join in the curse by agreeing with it. Once you do that, you've bound yourself to the curse.

An agreement is simply joining with a curse by letting it speak and hold power over you: *Mom's right, my thighs are gigantic.* And just like that, you begin a lifelong war with the size and shape of your thighs. This war is fueled by your self-contempt for a particular part of your body, in this case the adipose tissue surrounding your two femurs.

If you can notice where you have self-contempt for a particular part of your body, you can learn something about where you have been cursed. Which is to say, you can learn something about your story.

In this way, self-contempt *can become a compass for you.* It can take you to the very places in your story where you have been cursed. If you become aware of your self-contempt toward particular portions of your body, you will also become aware of stories of cursing. In short, your posture toward your body will reveal the truth of your story to you.

CHAPTER 8 **KEY POINTS**

- Your body will help you make sense of your story by communicating important truths through physical sensations, emotions, and impulses.
- Before you can listen to the wisdom of your body, you may need to restore trust in your body as a valid instrument of knowing.
- You have a relationship with the various parts of your physical body.
- You have likely experienced the cursing of particular parts of your body, which can make it very difficult to have a posture of kindness toward these parts of your body.

9

WHAT IF YOU EXPLORED YOUR COLLECTIVE/ CULTURAL STORY?

When it comes to race, the past is always present.
Michael Eric Dyson, *Tears We Cannot Stop*

The fundamental premise of story work is that your past story is affecting your present life. This is just as true for your *collective* story as it is for your individual story. Your day-to-day life is deeply affected by the past story of *the collective to which you belong.*

Most people belong to more than one collective. For example, if you are Korean American, you have at least three collective stories at play inside of you: the story of what it means to be Korean, the story of what it means to be American, and the story of what it means to be Korean American. All three of these cultural stories deeply affect the way your brain takes in the world.

Engaging your story means learning something about how each of these collective stories has shaped you. I am a White American. I can engage my family of origin story deeply, but if I don't explore what it means to be a White American, there is a ceiling on how much freedom and growth I will experience.

When I say "the past isn't dead," I am not merely referring to your individual past. I'm also referring to the cultural narratives you were born into. The sociological term for this is *social location*. You were born into a very particular social location.

Social location is fundamentally about *belongingness*. As you grow up in the world, you begin to learn where you belong and where you do not belong. The brain is highly attuned to this information because thousands of years ago, knowing which group you belonged to was a matter of life and death. We human beings are tribal creatures—which is to say that belonging to a particular collective or collectives *allows our nervous system to feel safe*.

Here's the dilemma: the collective story of some groups includes the exploitation and subjugation of other groups. Every culture contains deep goodness, and every culture contains deep sin.

As I am an American, the story of America is part of my collective story. The story of America bears great glory and great sin, just like the story of Mexico, Poland, and Thailand.

As I am also a White American, part of my collective story includes the White destruction of the original dwellers of this land and the exploitation of Black laborers to build White wealth. If you live in America, these aspects of our collective story have profound effects on your present life—whether you are White, Indigenous, Black, Asian, or Hispanic.

A central tenet of story work is that in order for healing to occur, there must be an honest naming of what has been true, an honest naming of *what actually happened*. This is true in your individual story and it is equally true in your collective story. As a White American, I have to name what has been true of my collective story—that is, I have to put honest words to what happened in America between White people and Indigenous people, as well as between White people and the peoples of Africa. A critical part of the story of White Americans is that we stole the land we now live on, destroyed the native inhabitants of America, and enslaved an untold number of Africans to produce wealth for us.

A wound that is unnamed is a wound that cannot heal.

On the whole, American society denies the existence of its own wound.

Denial is the opposite of naming; it is the opposite of confession. Many White people in America have yet to candidly name the impact of slavery on the present.

In chapter 2, I quoted Jeremiah 6:13–14 and 8:10–11, in which God rebukes the leaders of Israel for minimizing the wounds of the people:

> Prophets and priests alike,
>   all practice deceit.
> They dress the wound of my people
>   as though it were not serious.
> "Peace, peace," they say,
>   when there is no peace.

This is what the majority of White Christians in America are presently doing: we minimize the wounds of our BIPOC brothers and sisters. We say, "Peace, peace . . . everything is fine."

When people of color cry out, we attempt to silence their cries by replying, "Don't be divisive; don't let anger over past wrongs get in the way of unity today." This is precisely what angers the God of justice so deeply in Jeremiah.

Indeed, God's words to the leaders of Israel could be spoken to White Christians in America today: *we practice deceit.* We are dressing the wounds of our BIPOC brothers and sisters as though they are not serious. We continue to say "Peace, peace," when there are very real wounds in the hearts and bodies of our brothers and sisters.

Michael Eric Dyson wrote a book called *Tears We Cannot Stop: A Sermon to White America*. The entire book is Dyson *crying out* to White America. Dyson begins by saying, "Oh God, how we suffer.... We can do nothing to make our tormentors stop their evil."[1]

Am I really a tormentor just because I am White? Am I really doing evil? Either Dyson is engaged in accusatory hyperbole or I, as part of White America, have refused to honestly name something that is true.

Dyson's prayer continues in a very interesting vein. He cries out to God, saying, "How can we possibly combat the *blindness* of white men and women who are so deeply invested in their own privilege that they cannot afford *to see how much we suffer*?"[2] Finally, he concludes his prayer by saying, "Lord, convict this nation as never before.... Let this nation repent of its murderous ways."[3]

If you are White, what do you do with Dyson's plea? You have two choices: you can argue that Dyson is out of touch with reality and blowing things out of proportion, or you can grapple with the possibility that we White Americans have not repented of our murderous ways.

To be sure, Dyson is not saying anything new. For over four hundred years, Black people have been crying out—screaming, yelling, desperately pleading with White people to take their wounds seriously.

Consider the opening paragraph to *Race Matters* by Cornel West. These words have haunted me ever since I read them two decades ago.

---

1. Michael Eric Dyson, *Tears We Cannot Stop: A Sermon to White America* (New York: St. Martin's Press, 2017), 21.
2. Dyson, *Tears We Cannot Stop*, 21.
3. Dyson, *Tears We Cannot Stop*, 33.

> Black people in the United States differ from all other modern people owing to the unprecedented levels of unregulated and unrestrained violence directed at them. No other people have been taught systematically to hate themselves—psychic violence—reinforced by the powers of state coercion—physical violence—for the primary purpose of controlling their minds and exploiting their labor for nearly four hundred years. The unique combination of American terrorism—Jim Crow and lynching—as well as American barbarism—slave trade and slave labor—bears witness to the distinctive American assault on black humanity.[4]

If you are American, part of the collective story that courses through your veins is the story of the White American assault on BIPOC bodies.

This assault has not ended. Dyson says, "You cannot know what terror we live in."[5] He's not talking about the past; he's talking about today.

This assault on bodies of color has left deep and wide pools of innocent blood crying out from the ground. This blood is fully present today: it lies just beneath the ground we walk on as we go to work, take our kids to school, or enter our churches.

Anticipating the objections of White people, Dyson concludes, "If you claim that slavery and Jim Crow are ancient history . . . *how could that history be erased so quickly?*"[6]

Think about your family of origin story for a moment: If the past is present with regard to your personal story (if events that happened decades ago are still affecting you today), why would it be any different for our collective story as a nation?

---

4. Cornel West, *Race Matters* (Boston: Beacon Press, 1993), vii. Although the assault on Black humanity is distinctive, it is certainly not isolated. White America also assaults other non-White peoples, including Asian, Hispanic, and Indigenous peoples.

5. Michael Eric Dyson, "What White America Fails to See," *New York Times*, July 7, 2016, https://www.nytimes.com/2016/07/10/opinion/sunday/what-white-america-fails-to-see.html.

6. Dyson, *Tears We Cannot Stop*, 181–82.

Indeed, the past isn't dead; it's not even past. Each person in America is living in the midst of profound levels of racial trauma.

If you are a person of color, you know all too well that you experience racial trauma routinely as you live in a country built upon white supremacy and designed around whiteness. Moreover, you hold in your bodies and psyches and souls the knowledge of what your ancestors suffered at the hands of White people. As a result, many people of color feel an unsettledness in their bodies when they are around White people.[7]

If you are White, your body and psyche and soul carry the knowledge of what your ancestors did to the native inhabitants of this land as well as to Black people during slavery and Jim Crow. You live with the knowledge that your ancestors traumatized people of African descent for the purpose of dehumanization and subjugation. Moreover, you carry the knowledge of your *present* complicity in a society that continues to traumatize people of color.

To say it differently, White Americans carry immense shame inside our bodies, and we are often unaware that this shame is present. When we *are aware* of it, we frequently try to distance ourselves from it and/or deny that the shame is ours to grapple with.

The essence of trauma is *powerlessness* combined with *abandonment by potentially protective caregivers*. If you are a person of color, you experience these two hallmarks of trauma on a daily basis. First, you are confronted with the immense power differential between White people and people of color. Second, you feel the sting of abandonment as you watch White people daily abandon people of color by refusing to take action to establish justice in our land. In short, people of color experience *present* racial trauma much more frequently than White people like me want to admit.

---

7. Resmaa Menakem, *My Grandmother's Hands: Racialized Trauma and the Pathway to Mending Our Hearts and Bodies* (Las Vegas: Central Recovery Press, 2017), 15.

The healing of both people of color and White people is bound up in honestly addressing the immense harm that has been done. Yes, *even the healing of White people*. An Australian Aboriginal activist named Lilla Watson has often said to the White people in her midst, "If you have come to help us, you are wasting your time. But if you believe that *your liberation is bound up with ours*, let us work together."[8]

You and I are not here primarily to help those we have harmed. We are here because *our* liberation is bound up with their healing. When White Americans ignore the cries of our Black brothers and sisters for centuries, that indicates there is something deeply wrong with the hearts of White Americans. We are bound by something, and *our* liberation is tied to the liberation of our Black brothers and sisters.

WHERE TO START

The starting point of naming your collective story is *acknowledging you have a group to which you belong*. In other words, if you are White, you have to name that you are White and that "White people" is a racial group.

We White people have to acknowledge that we have been socialized into the collective of White people, and that socialization into whiteness has had a profound effect on the development of our brains. Socialization simply refers to the process of *internalizing the norms and beliefs of a group that you are part of*.

For those of us who are White, it can be very difficult to identify the ways we have been socialized by our whiteness, because whiteness is the norm. Since whiteness is the dominant culture

---

8. Though this quote has been attributed to Lilla Watson since her address at the 1985 United Nations Decade for Women Conference in Nairobi, Kenya, she is not comfortable being identified as the sole author, and has explained that in the early 1970s she was part of an Aboriginal rights group in Queensland, Australia, and together they came up with the phrase.

in America, many White people think we somehow escaped the process of being socialized into our race the way Black people and Asian people are.

As a White man, I have been socialized into whiteness—which means that I have internalized the norms and beliefs White people hold *as a group*. Because of the social nature of the brain, it is impossible *not* to internalize the norms and beliefs of the groups to which you belong.

You may be thinking to yourself, *But I'm an individual. I think for myself. I don't believe everything that other people of my race believe. Plus, I'm objective. I'm not biased.* Both of these notions—individualism and objectivity—are features of the Enlightenment. Individualism maintains that it is possible to be an independent thinker rather than taking on the beliefs of the group. Objectivity maintains that it is possible to be free from bias.

Here's the problem with individualism and objectivity: modern neuroscience demonstrates that both of these notions are false.

It is neurobiologically impossible to resist socialization into a collective, and it is neurobiologically impossible to be objective. The brain is a profoundly *social* organ—in other words, your brain has been shaped by the groups you are part of. And one of the groups you are part of is your racial group.

The first step for White people in engaging their collective story is to understand they have a race and have been socialized into whiteness. This is not a bad thing. It does not make them bad people. It simply means they have been profoundly shaped by whiteness.

For White people like me: your character is not a function of whether or not you have been shaped by white supremacy. Your character is a function of whether or not you are willing to look honestly at your collective story and how white supremacy has shaped your neural networks. The goal is not to be innocent. There is no innocence to be proven here.

WHAT IF YOU EXPLORED YOUR COLLECTIVE/CULTURAL STORY?

When I was twelve, I remember walking down our gravel driveway to get the mail with my dad. I was dragging my feet, and my dad sternly said to me, "Don't drag your feet like a . . ." and then he said the N word. What do you think that does inside the brain of a twelve-year-old boy?

I'd just been shamed by my father for dragging my feet. But my dad had also offered me a salve for that shame . . . a way to make the shame decrease. The way to make the shame decrease was to remind myself, *At least I'm not a Black person who drags their feet all the time*. And *just like that*, white supremacy put down roots in my young heart.

Fast-forward a few years. I'm sitting around the family dinner table, and the subject of affirmative action comes up. With equal parts anger and hurt, my dad says, "Affirmative action lets Black people have the promotion that I'm trying to get even though they haven't earned it. Affirmative action is a handout to Black workers who haven't earned the right to the promotion that should be mine. In short, someone less qualified than me is allowed to steal the job from me."

Now, what do you think happened inside my teenage brain as I listened to my dad express his hurt and anger? What do you think happened inside my heart as my hero (Dad) said that Black people were stealing jobs from White people? This dinner conversation is one of the ways I was *socialized into the idea that whiteness is better than blackness*. My brain was deeply influenced by my dad's convictions. And remember, he's my dad—as a fourteen-year-old boy, I did not yet have the context to say to myself, *Don't listen to Dad right now; he's expressing racist ideas*. Instead, I am going to perceive affirmative action as unfair, and I'm going to perceive Black people as stealing something from my dad.

At the time, there was no way for me to realize the absurdity of my dad's words. My dad was angry because a hypothetical Black person could hypothetically steal an opportunity from him. The reality is that my father's ancestors stole this Black man's ancestors from Africa and brought them to America (slave trade). Then they stole the fruit their work produced (slave labor). It was the legalized stealing of Black labor, Black ingenuity, Black creativity, Black business savvy—so that White people could enjoy the fruits of what Black people earned. My dad was angry about a Black person "stealing" what was rightfully his.

I hope you see the absurdity.

But as a fourteen-year-old boy, I didn't know any of that.

Because that's not how slavery was taught in my social studies textbook, which was written by White people who couldn't bear to be honest about the degree to which modern White wealth was created by Black people.

As a result, I was socialized into racist ideas about Black people.

Given what we know about how neurons operate, do you think these racist ideas simply disappeared from my brain as I grew into adulthood? Of course not.

Racist ideas are deeply ingrained in my brain. I have racist neural networks. That doesn't make me a horrible person. It makes me a person with neurons who grew up in America.

I am not the only White person with a brain bathed in white supremacy. If you grew up as a White person in America, then part of your collective story is based on white supremacy also. This doesn't make you a bad person; it simply means you have been paying attention to your environment and your neurons have been working.

All of our brains—whether White or BIPOC—have developed in the midst of a society that overwhelmingly privileges whiteness over all other skin tones. Even without a dad like mine, you can't grow up in America without being socialized into whiteness.

There is no easy way to address the harmful realities of our cultural stories. *Too much harm has been done.* However, each one of us can choose to look honestly at the past and acknowledge how the past is present—or (some of us can) try to ignore that the past is a powerful player in the present state of affairs.

Story work is based on the premise that the past affects the present. This is just as true with our cultural stories as it is with our family of origin stories. Story work is also based on the premise that healing requires an honest naming of what has happened in the past. And, again, this is just as true with our cultural stories as it is with our family of origin stories.

We must approach our cultural wounds the same way we approach physical wounds to our body: treating them with the utmost care as they are looked at, examined, and tended to.

Let me end with an important reminder for White people like me: your character is not a function of whether you have been shaped by white supremacy. Your character is a function of the degree to which you are willing to look honestly at your collective story and how white supremacy has shaped your neural networks.[9]

CHAPTER 9 **KEY POINTS**

- Both individual and collective stories influence your present-day life.
- To engage your story requires identifying the particular ways that you have been socialized into a racial group.
- Interpersonal shalom (see chapter 1) requires an honest acknowledgment of the barbaric harm done by white supremacy.
- The only alternative to an honest naming of past racial harm is denial of the past, which amounts to dressing the wounds of others as though they are not serious.

---

9. For an excellent, in-depth commentary on collective trauma in the United States, please read *My Grandmother's Hands* by Resmaa Menakem.

10

WHAT IF YOU EXPLORED YOUR STORY WITH GOD?

> You won't write a really glorious story until you've wrestled with the Author who has already written long chapters of your life, many of them not to your liking. We resist telling a story we don't like, and we don't like our own stories. But consider this: if you don't like your story, then you must not like the Author. Or conversely: if you love the Author, then you must love the story he has written in and for your life.
>
> Dan Allender, *To Be Told*

At the core of your heart is the history of how you have interacted with God about your desires and disappointments.[1] You may not like your story. Surely there are parts of it—perhaps entire seasons of your life—which you are not fond of. *Why did God let that happen? Why did God let my dad do that stuff to me? How could God have watched my mother treat me like*

---

1. Dan Allender, "Narrative Focused Trauma Care Certificate Program Lecture," Chicago, IL, 2013.

that? How could God stand by while the church—*of all places*—hurt me so deeply?

If you take your story seriously, if you take your heart seriously, if you take your wounds seriously—then sooner or later you will find yourself disoriented by the tragedies, heartaches, and betrayals that have happened to you. And the very fact that those stories of harm exist implicates God.

Job is the biblical example par excellence of someone whose life was turned upside down by tragedy and heartache. How did Job respond when his story took a massive turn for the worse? The answer is as simple as it is surprising. Job responded in two primary ways: lament and anger.

BIBLICAL LAMENT

Job's story was going along swimmingly when, all of a sudden, tragedy struck. He lost his wealth, his health, and his children. What were the first words he spoke after his world shattered?

> After this Job opened his mouth and cursed the day of his birth. And Job said:
>
> > "Let the day perish on which I was born,
> >   and the night that said,
> >   'A man is conceived.'
> > Let that day be darkness! . . .
> > Why did I not die at birth[?] . . .
> > For my sighing comes instead of my bread,
> >   and my groanings are poured out like water.
> > For the thing that I fear comes upon me,
> >   and what I dread befalls me." (Job 3:1–4, 11, 24–25 ESV)

Perhaps the most astonishing words in the above passage are *Job opened his mouth*. Job 3:1 says, "*After this* Job opened his mouth." After what? After he lost his children, his wealth, and his health.

After his wife told him to curse God and die. After his three friends came and sat in silence with him for seven days. After the silence, after the shock of the pain—as the horror of the pain was actually settling in—Job opened his mouth *and spoke*.

The first point I'd like to make is that Job didn't have to speak about his pain. He didn't have to engage with God. He could have taken his own life or killed himself in a different way—he could have *numbed* himself to his pain. Pushed his pain down into the basement of his heart. He could have disconnected from the reality of his life.

Job chose not to deny his pain. He chose not to deny or ignore his story, as awful as it was. He *spoke* about it. He put words to his emotional turmoil. He found language to express his internal reality. This is what it means to engage your story *with God*.

When your world is falling apart, will you open your mouth? Will you have the courage to express to God what you are truly feeling inside? If it feels too overwhelming to actually speak to God about your pain, what would it feel like to take a notebook and write out a prayer? It is an act of holy defiance to put words to the devastation and anguish in your heart. It is rebellion against the evil in our world that seeks to keep our pain hidden and to keep us isolated.

When Job opened his mouth and spoke, out came a lament. *Lament* is a passionate expression of sorrow, sadness, or grief. Lament is what comes out of you when your dreams are shattered. Job's heart was so tormented by his pain that his lament brought him to curse the day of his birth.

Job's story was so full of pain that the only thing that brought him comfort was wishing he had never been born in the first place.

When pain enters your life—whether it's small or large—what do you think is the *Christian response* to that pain? What should be your attitude when you're suffering? What are you supposed to do?

It's common to think,

> "I should ask God to increase my faith during this time," or
>
> "The ultimate reason I'm in so much pain is because I have made something in my life more important than God, and so I should repent," or
>
> "I should be grateful for what I still do have."

Job did none of that. In fact, each of those responses can be a way to *avoid* engaging your story. Each is a way to avoid being honest with God about your heartache and pain.

Job didn't ask God to increase his faith. He didn't repent of valuing his possessions or his health more than God. He didn't say, "I should be grateful for what I have left." Job wished he was dead. Job wished he had never been born because his sorrow and pain were overwhelming. Do you feel like a response like this is somehow ungodly?

The problem with this conclusion is that there is no shortage of biblical heroes who wished they were dead.

> Rebekah said, "I'm disgusted with living . . . my life will not be worth living" (Gen. 27:46).
>
> Moses asked God to "go ahead and kill [him]" (Num. 11:15).
>
> Elijah "prayed that he might die" (1 Kings 19:4).
>
> Jonah said, "Now, Lord, take away my life, for it is better for me to die than to live" (Jon. 4:3).
>
> And then there is Jeremiah, who uttered a lament quite similar to Job: "Cursed be the day I was born! . . . Why did I ever come out of the womb to see trouble and sorrow and to end my days in shame?" (Jer. 20:14, 18).

What's wrong with these people? Are they self-indulgent whiners drowning in a sea of self-pity? According to the Bible, it doesn't appear so. It appears that—for many people—wishing you were dead because you are overwhelmed by pain is part of life with God. It doesn't last forever, but it's real and it happens and there is nothing un-Christian about it—in fact, wanting to die is often part of the stories of people who really love God.

The laments that fill the book of Job (and there are plenty of them, along with laments in other parts of Scripture) give us *permission to feel*. And if you're a Christian, chances are you need that permission. Specifically, to feel your so-called negative emotions. If you are going to explore your story, you need to feel your anger, fear, and sadness.

What is keeping you from feeling these feelings?

What If You Prayed Your Feelings?

Not only does the book of Job give us permission to feel but it also gives us permission to talk with God—*candidly*—about our feelings. In other words, Job invites us to *pray* our feelings.

To pray your feelings is to pre-reflectively pour out your feelings to God.[2] *Pre-reflectively*—before you've reflected on your feelings and judged them as good or bad. To pray your feelings is to pour them out to God before *editing* your words.

When was the last time you just poured out your feelings to God without first making them "appropriate" for expression to a holy God or consistent with some sort of theology? More specifically: When was the last time you poured out your *sadness* to God?

If you are not regularly pouring out your anger, fear, and sadness to God, there is a *reason* for that. Nothing is more hardwired into the human heart than the tendency to run to someone bigger and stronger than you for help when you are in need. If you have

---

2. I am indebted to Tim Keller for this definition. Tim Keller, "Praying Our Tears," sermon, Redeemer Presbyterian Church, New York, February 27, 2000.

stopped doing this—if you have stopped running toward someone stronger than you and stopped expressing your sadness, fear, and anger—your story will help you understand why you have stopped. *Your story holds the reason.*

What do you need to begin running to God again and pouring out your feelings? You did this automatically as a five-year-old with your mom or dad (or you would have if they were available to you). When did you stop doing this with God?

In Job 3, we meet a man in a state of disorientation. Job's world has gone on tilt, and he expresses himself from this place of disorientation. He does not deny he's disoriented and can't figure out what's going on or even which way is up.

Many of us think we are living in a well-ordered and just world. A fair world.[3] And this carries us along for some time. But then something tragic happens—a life-threatening illness, the loss of a job, marriage problems, a betrayal by someone thought to be absolutely trustworthy—and what we thought of as a safe, fair world comes crashing down.

God's invitation to each of us in that moment is to lament. When the world as you understood it falls apart—when your story takes you down a road you do not wish to travel—*what if you expressed yourself to God in that moment?* What if you risked lament?

Lament consists of two things: (1) allowing yourself to feel your sorrow/grief/sadness, and (2) expressing that sorrow/grief/sadness.

We're reluctant to use the language of lament because it seems to be an expression of distrust in God rather than trust. We read Job saying, "Why did I not die at birth?" and we think, *A Christian shouldn't say things like this—who am I to question God?*

---

3. If you are a person of color and/or belong to a group that has been systematically oppressed, then you were likely disillusioned of this notion at a young age. But for those of us in dominant cultural groups, the illusion of a fair, well-ordered world often persists until tragedy strikes.

Isn't saying "God, I wish I were dead" evidence of one's distrust in God? My answer is no. What I'd like to suggest is that these words depict the anguish of a soul *yet are characteristic of a life of deep faith*. It takes more faith and trust to take your sorrow to God than it does to push down your true feelings or deny them.

The Purpose of Lament

If you've risked pouring out your sorrow and grief to God, you may have felt the nagging questions, What is the purpose of this? What's the goal? Doesn't lament just lead to more despair? If you are not regularly wrestling with God about your story, one of the reasons for that is likely because you lack confidence that any good will come from it.

But the path of lament need not lead to despair. Despair results when we lament *without hope*. The starting point of the story of Israel is the reversal of hopelessness. In Genesis 12:1–2, God said to Abraham, "Go from your country, your people and your father's household to the land I will show you. I will make you into a great nation." But a few verses earlier, in Genesis 11:30, we read, "Now Sarai [Abraham's wife] was barren. She had no child" (ESV). You can't become a great nation without procreating.

The story of Israel begins with *utter and complete hopelessness*: Sarah was barren. Old Testament scholar Walter Brueggemann puts it like this:

> Barrenness is the way of human history. It is an effective metaphor for hopelessness. . . . [But] the marvel of biblical faith is that barrenness is the arena of God's life-giving action. . . . After Sarah, Rebecca (25:21), Rachel (29:31), and Hannah (1 Sam. 1:2) were barren.[4]

---

4. Walter Brueggemann, *Genesis*, in Interpretation: A Bible Commentary for Teaching and Preaching, ed. by James L. Mays and Patrick D. Miller (Atlanta: John Knox Press, 1982), 116.

If "barrenness is the arena of God's life-giving action," we would expect God to immediately and miraculously give Sarah what she longs for—namely, pregnancy and a healthy baby. However, because the Bible is so relentlessly true to real life, chapters 12–14 of Genesis come and go and Sarah is still not pregnant. In other words, the promise of God *delays*... and Abraham and Sarah understandably enter a season of doubt.

Again, here is Brueggemann's commentary:

> It is part of the destiny of our common faith that those who believe the promise and hope against barrenness nevertheless must *live with the barrenness*. Why and how does one continue to trust solely in the promise when the evidence against the promise is all around? . . . *Can the closed womb of the present be broken open to give birth to a new future?* . . . The utter impossibility of the promise becomes evident. Abraham knows what is possible. He lives in restless torment.[5]

You may be at a point in your story where "the closed womb of the present" is all you can see. It's all you have lived. Perhaps for years. What would it feel like to let Brueggemann's question begin to pulse inside of you: *Can the closed womb of the present be broken open to give birth to a new future?*

If you give this question a little room to breathe inside—if you risk letting yourself hope for a moment—*your body* will naturally begin to engage God about the heartache of your present story. And if you risk letting your deepest parts engage with God, you will find Someone in the fire with you, in the heat.

More than wanting a particular circumstance to change, we want to feel the presence of Someone in the fire with us. We want to know—at an experiential level—that God's very self is with us in it. It is not pain we fear, it is aloneness and meaninglessness in the pain.

---

5. Brueggemann, *Genesis*, 140, 142–43. Emphasis mine.

Lamenting alone leads to despair. But lament poured out to God leads to something else. Eventually, it leads to connection with God and some measure of meaning in the pain (which in no way makes the pain "worth it").

Tears are a form of confession. They are the ultimate acknowledgment of what was—and is—true. They are the breakthrough of the (sometimes very long) denial of reality. But, as Walter Brueggemann reminds us, "embrace of ending permits beginnings . . . [for] only grievers can experience their experiences and move on."[6]

FEELINGS AS A WINDOW TO DESIRE

Have you stuffed your real feelings because you don't believe those feelings are consistent with a life of faith? Perhaps you feel a deep sadness rise up for a moment, and then you think, *I'm supposed to rejoice in the Lord always*, and so you pretend you're not full of sorrow, or you push the sorrow down to get it out of your awareness. Most of us are deeply uncomfortable with our big feelings. But *feelings are a window to the passionate desires of your heart*. Your feelings express something about who you are and what you want in life. Your feelings expose the rumblings of the deepest parts of your soul.

Neuroscience has demonstrated we are powerless to control our feelings. Feelings happen in a fraction of a second, before the executive control center of the brain (the part that makes volitional choices) comes online. God knows this. As the Creator of both your limbic system and your prefrontal cortex, God knows you cannot control that initial twinge of sadness or spike of anger. These emotional reactions are automatic and unconscious.

God does not call you to get rid of your sorrow or your anger or your fear; God calls you to *honesty* about your sorrow, anger, and fear.

---

[6]. Walter Brueggemann, *The Prophetic Imagination*, 40th anniversary ed. (Minneapolis: Fortress Press, 2018), 56, 57.

Sorrow

To deny sorrow is an odd inclination for people who value the Bible, given the large portions of its text in which people pour out their sorrow to God. Here is a small sampling from Psalms:

> My soul is in deep anguish. How long, Lord, how long? (6:3)
>
> Why, Lord, do you stand far off? Why do you hide yourself in times of trouble? (10:1)
>
> How long, Lord? Will you forget me forever? (13:1)
>
> My eyes fail, looking for your promise; I say, "When will you comfort me?" (119:82)

God has put these expressions of sorrow and despair into Scripture. Why would God have done that? Perhaps God wants you to give yourself permission to feel your real feelings and is inviting you to pour out those feelings to God in lament.

What if you engaged God with the same gritty, raw, honest energy that Job did? What if you brought your lament to God? What might happen? What might transpire in the few seconds, minutes, or days following your heartfelt, tear-filled, more-earnest-than-you've-ever-been speech to God?

There are two reasons lament can be very difficult.

1. When you risk connecting to your sorrow and putting words to it, you begin to feel even *more* of the sadness in your heart. Last year I worked with a woman who was functionally kicked out of her church community just as she was stepping into her gifting and taking on a new leadership role. Three of the church elders turned on her, expressed their "concerns about her leadership style," and said that the church would no longer support her ministry. As this woman poured out her sadness to God about the

present situation, she began to connect with sorrow in her heart that predated the betrayal of those three elders. This is very common. Why? *Because our stories are linked.* That's how neurons operate. Neurons that fire together, wire together. So, when you take the risk of feeling your sorrow about something in your forties, it will likely connect you to sorrow that your body holds from your teens and twenties.

2. Expressing sorrow often connects you to the agony of the *powerlessness* you also feel. The more this woman felt her sorrow, the more she realized how unable she was to prevent the betrayal from happening. One of the reasons we don't want to feel our sorrow is because it connects us to this very unpleasant feeling of powerlessness.

Maybe you resonate with one of these reasons, or maybe you have a different reason for avoiding lament. If you are reluctant to express your sorrow to God, can you begin by simply talking to God about that resistance?

Anger

Sorrow is not the only feeling we keep at bay. Many of us also keep anger at bay. Especially anger at God.

You may not *feel* angry at God, but I'll bet the anger is there, lurking below the surface. Perhaps you grew up in a religious culture in which it was considered flat-out wrong to feel anger at God. It was wrong to ever feel abandoned by God. It was wrong to ever feel disappointed in God. As a result, if you find yourself feeling even the littlest bit of anger at God or disappointment in God, you immediately nip that feeling in the bud because you believe it is somehow ungodly or wrong to feel that way.

If you risk talking candidly with God about your story—expressing your real feelings—there will be times when you may feel abandoned by God. Perhaps you feel abandoned by God in a particular moment in your story. *How could you have let me be sexually abused? Why didn't you prevent it? Why didn't you make my family move into a different neighborhood so that the boy who abused me would never have been in my life? Would that have been so hard, God? For you to have me live in a slightly different neighborhood?*

Or you might feel abandoned by God *in the present* as you try to heal from your wounds . . . and your efforts to find healing don't seem to be working.

I have personally felt a great deal of anger at God. And I still do in many ways. I'm angry at God that I was born into a home with a deeply broken mother who sexualized our relationship daily. I'm angry at God that I was born into a home with a war-traumatized father who refused to get help. I'm angry at God that it took me so long to find someone who could help me heal from my own pain.

If you are emotionally honest, sooner or later you will feel anger toward God.

What does your anger at God tell you *about you*?

More often than not, your anger at God is a result of how important God is to you. It's evidence of your holiness, of your faithfulness to God. Bear with me as we return to Job's story. Job began feeling—and expressing—a great deal of anger at The One Who Could Have Stopped the Tragedy. Consider these words from Job 9 and 10.

> And Job spoke out and he said:
> Of course, I knew it was so:
>   how can man be right before God?
> Should a person bring grievance against Him,
>   He will not answer one of a thousand.
> Wise in mind, staunch in strength,
>   who can argue with Him and come out whole? . . .
> Look, He passes over me and I do not see,
>   slips by me and I cannot grasp Him.

> Look, He seizes me—who can resist Him? . . .
> And yet, as for me, I would answer Him,
>   would choose my words with Him.
> Though in the right, I can't make my plea.
>   I would have to entreat my own judge.
> Should I call out and He answer me,
>   I would not trust Him to heed my voice.
> Who for a hair would crush me
>   and make my wounds many for naught. . . .
> I shall say to God: Do not convict me.
>   Inform me why You accuse me.
> Is it good for You to oppress,
>   to spurn Your own palms' labor. . . .
> Your hands fashioned me and made me,
>   and then You turn round and destroy me! . . .
> If I offended, You kept watch upon me
>   and of my crime would not acquit me. . . .
> Like a triumphant lion You hunt me. . . .
> You summon new witnesses against me
>   and swell up Your anger toward me. . . .
> My days are but few—let me be.
>   Turn away that I may have some gladness. (Job 9:1–4, 11–12, 14–17; 10:2–3, 8, 14, 16–17, 20)[7]

There it is. A tour de force of rage directed unapologetically at The One Who Could Have Prevented It All.

Notice the particularity of Job's rage. What was he so angry about? First and foremost, Job was angry that *God was not responsive to his plea for help.*

Job said, "Should a person bring grievance against Him, He will not answer one of a thousand" (9:3). Job's point is that we can throw up a thousand prayers to God—a thousand grievances—and God won't answer a single one. Can you relate to this? I sure can. I bring

---

7. Robert Alter, *The Wisdom Books: Job, Proverbs, and Ecclesiastes: A Translation with Commentary* (New York: W. W. Norton, 2011), 42–50.

a grievance to God over and over and hear nothing back. And it is the deafening silence that is so disturbing... and so infuriating.

Second, Job was angry that God wouldn't respond to his complaint. Thus, Job said, "Should I call out and He answer me, I would not trust Him to *heed* my voice" (v. 16, emphasis mine). In other words, "In the unlikely event that God actually answers me, God won't heed my voice—God won't pay attention to what I am actually saying. God won't address the cause of my upset." This is the crux of Job's pain—Job wanted God to *respond* to the cries of his heart.

Third, Job was furious that God wounded him, and for no good reason: You "crush me and make my wounds many for naught" (v. 17). In other words, "God, you wound me over and over... and for what?"

In case you think that Job was simply having a bad day when he wrote chapters 9–10, it's important to know that as the book of Job unfolds, his anger increases rather than decreases. Here is a sampling of Job's anger in the upcoming chapters:

> You slay me.
>
> You write bitter things against me.
>
> You destroy my hope.
>
> You tear me apart.
>
> You shake me to pieces.
>
> You rush at me like a warrior.
>
> You strip from me my glory.
>
> You distance my brothers from me.
>
> You scheme against me.
>
> You deny me justice.

Some of us may be thinking, *Just because Job expresses all this anger at God doesn't mean it's right to do that. After all, Scripture is filled with examples of people doing the wrong thing.* Here's the problem with that: in the final chapters of the book of Job, God speaks. And one of the things God speaks about is the rightness of Job's words:

> And it happened after the LORD had spoken these words to Job, that the LORD said to Eliphaz the Temanite: "My wrath has flared against you and your two companions because *you have not spoken rightly of Me as did My servant Job.* And now, take for yourselves seven bulls and seven rams and go to My servant Job, and offer a burnt-offering for yourselves, and Job My servant will pray on your behalf. To him only I shall show favor, not to do a vile thing to you, for *you have not spoken rightly of Me as did my servant Job.*" (Job 42:6–8)[8]

What do we do with this passage? God said—twice—that Job had "spoken rightly" of God. Now, what in the world can that mean? Was God acknowledging that God tore Job apart and rushed at him like a warrior and made his wounds many for no good reason? I don't think so. So, what could it possibly mean that Job spoke rightly of God?

It means that *it was right for Job to express his anger at God.*

It was right for Job to bring his truest heart before God. It was right for Job to speak to God with unedited words.

It's important to understand that the story didn't have to go like this. Job didn't have to bring his anger to God. Job could have written God off. He could have said to himself, *God is not going to listen to me, and certainly won't answer. Therefore, I'm not going to waste my time yelling at God.* Boy, can I relate to that sentiment. In the very moments when I most need God to hear my anger and respond to me, I often feel like God is the least responsive. It can feel like I'm talking to the ceiling.

It is difficult to summon the courage to express anger at God. I still remember the first time I did so. When my torrent of rageful

---

8. Alter, *Wisdom Books*, 177. Emphasis mine.

words finally came to an end, I braced myself for God's retaliatory strike. Part of me was afraid God was going to smite me then and there. But was God really unaware of my deep anger until I spoke it aloud? Of course not.

Here's the thing: God can handle your anger. God is neither *surprised* by it nor *afraid* of it.

When you feel like God has let you down, will you allow yourself to feel anger? Just to feel it? And then will you take the risk of expressing to God what you are truly feeling inside?

Job is not the only person in the Bible to yell at God. The psalmists do it. A lot. We also see the writer of Lamentations cry out, "The Lord is like an enemy" (2:5). And lest you think this is merely an exaggerated simile, consider these words from Lamentations 3:

> God has driven me away and made me walk in darkness
>   rather than light; indeed, he has turned his hand
>   against me again and again. . . .
> He has besieged me and surrounded me with bitterness
>   and hardship. . . .
> Even when I call out or cry for help, he shuts out my
>   prayer. . . .
> Like a bear lying in wait, like a lion in hiding, he dragged
>   me from the path and mangled me and left me without
>   help.
> He drew his bow and made me the target for his arrows.
> He pierced my heart with arrows from his quiver. (3:2–3,
>   5, 8, 10–13)[9]

And then there is Psalm 44:

> [God,] you no longer go out with our armies.
> You made us retreat before the enemy. . . .

---

9. Robert Alter, *The Hebrew Bible: A Translation with Commentary*, Kindle ed. (New York: W. W. Norton, 2018).

> You *gave us up* to be devoured like sheep....
> All this came upon us,
> > though we had not forgotten you....
> Our hearts had not turned back....
> But you *crushed us*...
> > you covered us over with deep darkness. (vv. 9–11, 17–19, emphasis mine)

Do you really think these people were *quietly* saying all of this? Job, the psalmist, the author of Lamentations—these people are yelling at God.

It is surprising so many modern people deny anger at God, given the large number of biblical passages where people rage at God. God has put all these expressions of anger into Scripture. Why would God have done that?

I imagine someone is thinking, *Yes, some psalms begin with anger, but then the writer goes on to express trust in God.* This is often true. However, how much time do you think passed between the writing of Psalm 13:1 ("How long, Lord? Will you forget me forever? How long will you hide your face from me?") and the writing of verse 5 ("But I trust in your unfailing love; my heart rejoices in your salvation")?

One week? One month? One year? We think of David as writing an entire psalm in one sitting. Yet anyone who writes poetry or music knows that rarely happens. What if the place David found himself for an entire year was verse 1—"How long, Lord? Will you forget me forever? How long will you hide your face from me?"—before he was able to say, "But I trust in your unfailing love"?

UNTIL WE HAVE FACES

Anger is a very difficult emotion for many people, especially those of us with a history of trauma. For example, if most of the anger you witnessed as a child was dangerous and destructive, you may be very reluctant to actually feel the full weight of the anger inside. I've worked with plenty of people who have said, "I'm scared of what I would do if I felt all of my anger." Others have said, "Whenever I allow myself to feel my anger and express it, I hurt the people around me." The dilemma is your anger *cannot be quarantined*. If you have anger, it is leaking out in ways you are likely unaware of. The best way to assure it does not harm those you love is to welcome your anger, get to know it, and express it well.

Acknowledging your anger and expressing it will introduce you to yourself. It will allow you to become more connected to the truth of the heartbreak of your story. Your anger can lead you to get to know yourself better and to know your story better.

C. S. Lewis wrote a fairy tale called *Till We Have Faces*. The main character, Orual, feels wronged by the gods, and at the end of the book she finally gets an audience with them. Orual verbalizes her complaint against the gods—she yells at them for how they have mistreated her. When she's finished, she goes through the whole thing again. And then she says this:

> When the time comes to you at which you will be forced at last to utter the speech which has lain at the centre of your soul for years ... you'll not talk about joy of words. I saw well why the gods do not speak to us openly, nor let us answer. Till that word can be dug out of us, why should they hear the babble that we think we mean? How can they meet us face to face till we have faces?[10]

I love that. What is she saying? Lewis wrote a letter to a friend in which he explained what he was trying to say through Orual:

> The idea was that a human being must become real before it can expect to receive any message from [God]; that is, it must be speaking

---

10. C. S. Lewis, *Till We Have Faces: A Myth Retold* (New York: HarperOne, 2017), 335. Copyright © 1956 C. S. Lewis Pte. Ltd. Extract reprinted by permission.

with its own voice (not one of its borrowed voices), expressing its actual desires.[11]

Do you know what you're really angry with God about, deep down? What is the "speech which has lain at the centre of your soul for years"? Is it that God left you alone? Is it that God really doesn't seem to be there for you? What is your real *complaint* against God?

Maybe one of the reasons you are reluctant to continue looking at the heartache in your story is because you're afraid of what it's going to do to your relationship with God. But how can God meet you face-to-face until you have a face? How can God respond to the deepest cry of your soul until you have become clear about what that cry is and how—in your story—that cry came to be?

Years ago I wrote a poem about fighting with God, titled after the place where God wrestled with Jacob (see Genesis 32).

Jabbok

Why don't you come down here
in angelic form and
fight me like you fought Jacob?
Is it because you are afraid of my anger?
You alone know its intensity—
my capacity to erupt and desecrate.

Meet me at Jabbok
I will press your face into the earth—and beneath the earth.
You will choke on dirt, gasping for breath.

There is nothing ordinary about this fight—
no rounds, no retreating to your corner
for rest and instruction.
A coach can say nothing that applies here.

---

[11]. C. S. Lewis, "Letter to Dorothea Conybeare," in *C. S. Lewis: A Companion and Guide*, ed. by Walter Hooper (San Francisco: HarperCollins, 1996), 252. Copyright © 1996 C. S. Lewis Pte. Ltd. Extract reprinted by permission.

> This is not about tactics or strategy—I have none.
> All I bring is sheer raw rage.
>
> Why wrestling? Why not jousting or boxing
> or an adolescent fistfight?
> Because as the side of your head is
> pressed into the cold, dank earth
> I want to be right there, up close,
> to hear your labored breathing
> and feel your desperation.
>
> We would claw and scrape in moonlit shadows
> until the dark night gives way to dawn.
> Sitting motionless on the ground, exhausted,
> our fragile backs would lean against two ancient boulders
> while our heads—cushioned by thick sweat-drenched
>   hair—
> rest gently on crevices created for this moment.

It took me a long time to write this poem. But, more importantly, it took me a long time to enact this poem—in other words, to have my fight with God. What would it look like for you to get into the ring with God?

Your disappointment and pain are not small. They merit candid expression to the God who is so important to you. Moreover, you may find that the faithful expression of your genuine big feelings allows those feelings to move through your body in a way that brings newfound rest and settledness.

CHAPTER 10 KEY POINTS

- Your story likely includes seasons of deep pain and disappointment. One way to let that pain and disappointment move through you is to take the risk of genuinely expressing them to God.

- The biblical practice of lament allows you to connect with your true emotions and give voice to your sorrow and grief.
- Although it may feel scary to express your anger to God, it is an act of honesty and integrity that is essential for a genuine relationship with the divine.

11

WHAT IF YOU EXPLORED YOUR STORY WITH KINDNESS?

> We are not meant to enter the dark waters of memory without the presence of comfort and care.
>
> Dan Allender, *Healing the Wounded Heart*

A year of kindness toward your own heart will take you further on the healing journey than a year of weekly therapy with your dream therapist.[1] This is not a jab at the counseling profession; it is an observation about the power of self-kindness to evoke change in the human heart.

Here is a gut-wrenching truth about the by-product of trauma: the harm you do to yourself through self-contempt is greater than the harm that has been done to you. By "self-contempt" I simply mean harshness *from you to you*. The opposite of self-contempt is kindness.

---

1. This is equally true within a smaller time frame. If one year feels too ambitious, please know that even twenty minutes of kindness toward your own heart will bear more fruit than twenty minutes with a skilled therapist.

How do you know if you experience self-contempt? Answering the following questions may help.

> What is your posture toward yourself when you make a mistake or do something wrong?
>
> What do you say to yourself when you harm another person?
>
> What do you feel about yourself when you see something unlovely about your own heart or character?
>
> What is your posture toward yourself when you are not doing well?
>
> How do you respond to yourself when you are in a fight with your partner?
>
> When you think back to yourself as a ten-year-old, what is your posture toward that child? How do you *feel* toward them?
>
> When you think back to yourself as a fourteen-year-old, what do you think about that teen?

Self-contempt blocks the healing process more than any other single factor.

The antidote to self-contempt is *kindness*. According to the apostle Paul, it is the kindness of God that leads to repentance (see Rom. 2:4). If that's true, why does a part of you feel like the best way to change and grow is to be harsh with yourself? When you consider being kinder to yourself, what fears come up? What are you afraid might happen if you were kinder to yourself for the remainder of today?

If you're like me, you likely have difficulty with kindness... either receiving kindness from others or being kind to your own heart and body. Or perhaps both.

Consider the following two diagnostic questions. First, What's it like for you when someone gives you a genuine compliment?

Second, How do you tend to respond internally? For example, suppose someone says to you—with authentic delight—"You are really good at making people feel welcomed and included."

What happens inside of you as you hear those heartfelt words? Are you able to receive those words—to really let them echo in your heart, and then say a genuine thank-you as both of you share in the delight of your gifting? When someone is truly delighting in you, it can be very hard to receive their delight. To let it in.

Perhaps you think, *I don't want to be prideful*. A truer statement would be, "I can't bear it when your eyes see my goodness and glory. I can't bear you delighting in me like this. And so I'm not going to let your words fill my heart. Instead, I'm going to think of some way in which your words aren't true or find some way to deflect them."

We deflect by saying things to ourselves like *Well, so-and-so doesn't feel welcomed by me*, or *Well, it's not really me; God made me like this*.

Here's another question to help you ponder if you have difficulty receiving kindness: What is it like for you to be *celebrated*? How do you feel when someone throws a party for your birthday or gives you an extravagant gift?

For my thirty-fifth birthday, my wife gave me a present. It was a rectangle and looked like the box that a dress shirt might be in, except it was too heavy. As I began to open the present, I saw the pristine packaging of an Apple MacBook Pro. When I realized what it was, something in my body recoiled. I couldn't receive it. I literally *pushed the box away from me* and closed my eyes and said, "No, I don't think so."

What was going on there? I couldn't bear someone delighting in me *that* much. *A MacBook Pro as a birthday present?! Those things cost thousands of dollars. For me?*

What happens inside you when someone is truly delighting in you? What's it like for you when someone offers you kindness . . . even extravagant kindness (like a MacBook Pro)? Can you receive their delight in you?

Conversely, what's it like for you when you are in *need* of kindness? Is it easy to ask a close friend or your partner for care and support? When you are struggling emotionally—when you're having a bad day—what is your *posture* toward yourself?

For many of us, when we're not doing well, we tend to get angry at ourselves about it. In other words, in those moments when we are *most in need* of care and soothing, we are usually the most harsh with ourselves. It's this sense of, *Why am I so upset about this? Why am I letting that person get under my skin again? Why am I still worrying about money?*

When you are anxious or afraid, what do you tend to say to yourself? Do you have a posture of, *This is because I don't trust God enough. If I had faith like so-and-so, I wouldn't be so anxious and afraid all the time*? If words like these are familiar to you, then you know something about self-contempt. And notice something: it's not merely self-contempt—it's self-contempt *in the precise moment when you are most in need of care and kindness*.

How is it that you are harshest with yourself when you are most in need of care and comfort? Perhaps it has something to do with your immense *need* for kindness and your deep ambivalence about receiving kindness.

When you get dysregulated—when your body floods with cortisol—what do you notice about your posture toward your suffering body? When I get dysregulated, sometimes I chastise myself for being weak, for not being more mature than I am. How is it that my dysregulation becomes the occasion for me to accuse myself of not having grown enough?

Here's the point: self-contempt blocks your body from healing. *What if you began to explore your story with kindness rather than self-contempt?*

What if the process of exploring your story actually led to an increased ability to access self-kindness and a decrease in your levels of self-contempt?

There is a symbiotic relationship between story engagement and kindness—the more you are able to engage your story *with kindness*, the more of your story you will uncover. Similarly, the more you *engage your story*, the more kindness you will have access to. They are mutually reinforcing. They grow in tandem.

Do you want more access to your story? Risk being kinder with yourself. Do you want more self-kindness in your day-to-day life? Risk uncovering more and more about your story as a child.

There is a very poignant Carl Jung quote that exposes the pull to self-contempt that many people experience. Jung writes,

> That I feed the hungry, that I forgive an insult, that I love my enemy in the name of Christ, all these are undoubtedly great virtues. What I do to the least of my brethren, that I do unto Christ. But what if I should discover that the least among them all, the poorest of all the beggars, the most impudent of all the offenders—that these are *within me and that I myself stand in need of the alms of my own kindness*—that I myself am the enemy that must be loved—what then? As a rule, the Christian's attitude is then reversed; there is no longer the question of any love or compassion; we say to the brother within us, "You fool," and condemn and rage against ourself.[2]

What is Jung saying? First of all, we each have a relationship with ourselves. Let's start with that. Many Christians don't want to admit they have a relationship with themselves. Why? Because it feels self-centered, self-indulgent, or self-absorbed. The reasoning goes like this: *I'm supposed to be thinking of others, not myself.*

---

2. Carl Jung, *Psychology of Religion: East and West*, vol. 11 of *The Collected Works of C. G. Jung*, trans. by R. F. C. Hull (Princeton: Princeton University Press, 2024), para. 520. Emphasis mine.

But, like it or not, you *do* have a relationship with yourself. You can't not.

What do I mean by "a relationship with yourself"? I mean that at every moment of your day, you have a particular *posture* toward your own heart and body.

Over the course of your day, you are constantly engaged in dialogue with your own heart. You can't avoid this. Why? Because God created you with a *default mode network* in your brain. This is a group of brain structures that run along the midline of your brain. One job of this network is to enable you to think about yourself.

But many Christians believe that thinking about themselves is a bad thing. It's not a bad thing; *it's a human thing.* If God made your brain with a default mode network, God must have an interest in you spending some of your time thinking about your heart, your mind, your body . . . yourself.

So, you have a relationship with yourself.

How would you describe the *dynamics* of your relationship with yourself?

If I asked you to describe the dynamics of your relationship with your spouse or your boss or your best friend, you could put some words to the nature of those particular relationships. But what characterizes your relationship with *yourself*? Would you describe that relationship as warm? Affectionate? Or is it harsh or conflicted?

The second point Jung makes is that most Christians believe they are called to be kind and compassionate to the hurting, the needy, the suffering. And Jung basically says, "Okay, great . . . but what happens when the hurting person is *you*?" What's your stance toward "the hurting person" then? What happens when the needy one *is you*?

For many of us, our posture quickly becomes contemptuous.

When I am the hurting person, I am often not kind toward myself. I can be far kinder and more compassionate toward others in pain than I am toward myself in pain. Many of us are kinder to our friends when they are hurting than we are toward ourselves when we are hurting. Why? Perhaps it has something to do with our resistance to receiving kindness, particularly kindness to ourselves. One of the by-products of trauma is a war with kindness.

Engaging your story has as much to do with your posture toward yourself in the present as it does with looking at your past.

Why? Because, again, your past *is* present. Your past story is playing itself out in your present life today. This afternoon.

Have you ever considered why it's so hard to bring kindness to your own heart and body? Might it have something to do with what happened in your past when you were in need of kindness and care . . . and you were either shamed for that need or abandoned in your moment of need?

Think back on your growing-up years. How did your parents respond to you when you were in need—when you were feeling hopeless or overwhelmed or upset? Were you shamed for having needs? Were you left alone when you needed the care and comfort of an adult?

Why not begin to write a new story? You can begin by offering your heart and body kindness today when you are in need.

The real question is this: Are you *willing* to bring soothing, care, and comfort to your body when it is dysregulated?

For me, it can be quite hard to do so. Why? Because I'm mad at myself for being dysregulated. I'm mad at my body for being so affected by whatever has upset me. *Why does this person affect me so much? Why is this situation upsetting me so much?*

It is very common for people with a history of trauma to be at war with their dysregulated and emotionally activated bodies.

Dan Allender often says, "The hard work of life is not 'dealing with your pain.' The hard work of life is allowing yourself to experience comfort and kindness—from others and from yourself."

As counterintuitive as that sounds, I have found it to be very true. It is hard to allow myself to experience comfort and kindness.

The word *comfort* comes from the Latin prefix *com*, meaning "with," and the root *fortis*, meaning "strong." In other words, comfort is being *with* someone (*com*) to *strengthen* them (*fort*). To comfort means to be with someone out of a desire to strengthen them.

Anytime someone is truly *with you*, you are strengthened. It's axiomatic. When someone is truly with you, you can't help but be strengthened.

When someone is *with* you, it does not mean they understand you completely. It means they have the courage to enter your hurt because they have a *desire* to hear you and to understand you. And it means they have the kindness to be with you in a way that is both strong and tender.

Kindness is very different from niceness. A nice person will listen and perhaps say something in an attempt to be supportive or encouraging. However, the words of a nice person will rarely penetrate, disrupt, or provoke. In short, a nice person is more concerned with "not upsetting you" than with inviting you into a more repentant and redemptive way of living. When Proverbs 27:6 says "Wounds from a friend can be trusted," the writer is referring to the actions of a friend who risks kindness. If you are in need of care, and you are with someone who is merely nice, nothing can make you feel more alone.

Niceness does not strengthen us. Kindness strengthens by simultaneously providing genuine comfort and inviting us to become more fully ourselves.

OFFERING KINDNESS TO YOURSELF

As you explore your story, it will be important to grow in kindness toward yourself. Bringing comfort to yourself is a skill that can be learned. In many ways, this is merely an invitation to offer the Big Six *to yourself*. What is your posture toward yourself? I'm asking you to consider:

1. Are you *attuned to yourself*? Are you aware when you are in pain?
2. Are you emotionally *responsive to yourself* when you are having a hard time?
3. Do you *engage your own heart* when you are suffering?
4. Do you attempt to *regulate your own affect* when you are dysregulated?
5. When you are not doing well, do you give yourself *permission to feel* your negative emotions?
6. Do you *seek to repair* when you do harm to your own heart and body with self-contempt?

As Dan Allender puts it, "You don't have to respond to your story by joining in violence against yourself. You can respond to your story the way God does—with kindness, even kindness toward your frailty."

Why do we have contempt for our own frailty? Our own brokenness?

In Isaiah 42:3, God says, "A bruised reed [I] will not break." You and I are bruised reeds. **This is not a problem.** If God does not hate the fact that you are a bruised reed, why do *you*? Why do you have hatred for your brokenness, for your weakness, for your frailty?

When you are not doing well, do you respond to your body's suffering by striving harder? Grinding it out? Do you turn against yourself? You don't have to respond to your brokenness with all manner of self-accusations. Accusations are a form of self-violence.

You don't have to respond to your story by joining in violence against yourself.

What is keeping you from responding to your heart and body with kindness rather than contempt? With kindness rather than striving? With kindness rather than enduring?

It's important to understand that kindness, in and of itself, will begin to disrupt the power of evil in your day-to-day life.

Have you made a list of those things that bring your body a sense of calm, soothing, and comfort? What music calms you? What music makes your body feel good feelings? Have you made a playlist? And if you have, will you be kind enough to your body the next time it is dysregulated to listen to that soothing music?

Engaging your own story is as much about tending to your dysregulated body as it is about writing out the pivotal stories of your childhood.

Here's the dilemma: when we begin to treat ourselves with kindness rather than contempt, it awakens our unmet longings for good care and comfort. When we begin to get a taste of something we have experienced very little of, it rouses our longing for more.

We don't want to bring kindness, care, and comfort to our own bodies because we don't want to get connected to how much longing we have in this area. *We don't want to feel the ache of unmet need.*

And, for some of us, the desire for comfort and care actually brings a sense of humiliation. Why? Because if you let yourself feel your need for comfort, it means you actually have needs. And you may have a felt sense that being needy is a bad thing, a shameful thing.

RECEIVING KINDNESS FROM OTHERS

You may not be fond of this fact, but God designed you to need care. It's how the human heart is built. Created in the image of a triune God (a *we*, not an *I*), we are hardwired to need other people to provide comfort, care, and kindness when we are hurting.

Are you at war with the way God designed you? If so, have you pondered why this is the case?

For many people with a history of trauma, the person who offered you kindness, care, and comfort was often the same person who abused you. This is a nauseating truth.

It needs to be said again: for many people with a history of trauma, the person who offered you kindness, care, and comfort was often the same person who abused you.

Therefore, receiving another's comfort will feel way too close to how you were groomed by your abuser. As we mentioned earlier, your abuser cared for you in ways that made you become emotionally connected to them and trust them. This grooming process of offering kindness/care/comfort is the very thing that set you up for abuse.

As a result, your brain has paired kindness/care/comfort with "Something bad is about to happen to me." Therefore, when someone is kind to you now—in the present—you know in your gut there has to be a catch. *What does this person want from me? What is going to be asked of me or required from me?*

Do you see the dilemma? What the human heart most needs is kindness, but your brain has paired kindness with harm. So, now you are suspicious of kindness—even if you don't want to be. Indeed, your body has become suspicious of something that is good for you.

Think about it: When do you tend to turn against your heart? When are you tempted to join evil in accusations against yourself? It's not primarily when you are hurting. Rather, as Dan Allender has pointed out to me, it is when you are hurting *and there is the possibility of comfort*—comfort that you don't know what to do with because it reminds you too much of something nauseating in your story.

How does healing happen? In the end it is not truth that changes people; it is kindness. This is why a year of kindness toward your own heart will take you further on the healing journey than a year of great therapy.

Again, kindness, in and of itself, will begin to disrupt the ways evil has assaulted you. And when evil is disrupted, the body naturally heals. The more we engage our stories with kindness, the more our brains seem to change. The more we are open to receiving comfort from others and from ourselves, the more our brains seem to change.

What is most keeping you from offering kindness to yourself when you are struggling? Write it down here:

_____

_____

_____

CHAPTER 11 KEY POINTS

- Kindness toward yourself will take you further on the healing journey than you think.
- When you feel distressed or in need of care, it can be very difficult to receive kindness, especially if you have a history of harm.
- You may feel caught between your desire for comfort and your fear that others won't come through for you.
- The bottom line is that kindness—both toward oneself and from others—is crucial for healing past experiences of harm.

12

YOUR WAR WITH HOPE

> The very least you can do in your life is to figure out what you hope for. And the most you can do is to live inside that hope. Not admire it from a distance, but live right in it, under its roof.
>
> Barbara Kingsolver, *Animal Dreams*

One of the reasons you do not want to explore your story more deeply is because doing so will invariably catapult you into a war with hope. My thesis is that engaging your story will benefit you. That it will catalyze breakthrough in your life in precisely those places where you are the most stuck, feel the most helplessness, and have the most longing. However, each time you make a decision to explore your story—in big ways or small ways—you are forced to grapple with the hope and hopelessness that live inside of you.

You have hoped before. You have hoped for healing before. And that hope has propelled you to *do something*—read a particular book, attend a conference, go to therapy. Anticipation, infused with some measure of hope, made you think that perhaps *this will be the thing* to bring you breakthrough and healing.

Some of your attempts to find healing have been fruitful. However, some of your efforts have been like those of a farmer who planted a crop that did not yield a harvest. You took the time and did the work. *And then you risked letting yourself hope.* You hoped your labor would produce the fruit of healing. But no healing came. The harvest was not.

WHAT IS HOPE?

Psalm 27:13–14 says this:

> I remain confident of this:
> > *I will see the goodness of the* Lord
> > *in the land of the living.*
>
> *Wait* for the Lord;
> > be strong and take heart
> > and *wait* for the Lord. (emphasis mine)

There is a relationship between hope and waiting. In fact, the bodily experience of hope is very similar to the felt experience of waiting. If you are hoping for something, *you don't have it yet.* Therefore, you're waiting for it. But hope is not merely waiting. There is another element to it. Hope involves *groaning.* Groaning from the inside. Longing for something. Hope is *groaning inwardly while waiting expectantly.* Both. Hope is groaning—longing for something—while, at the same time, expecting it to happen.

And that is very hard to do.

Nietzsche said that hope is "the worst of all evils, because it prolongs the torments of man."[1] What torment is Nietzsche talking about? The torment of longing for something *that is never going to come to fruition.*

Think about your own life. There is something you want—a graduate degree, a child, your dad to actually be a dad. You've wanted

---

1. Friedrich Nietzsche, *Human, All Too Human (Parts One and Two)*, trans. by Helen Zimmern and Paul V. Cohn (Mineola, NY: Courier Corporation, 2012), 53.

it for years, and you've done everything you can to get it, but you still have not received it.

> Isn't it foolish to hope that this year you'll get into graduate school?
>
> Isn't it silly to hope that next month you'll conceive a child?
>
> Isn't it stupid to hope that this afternoon your dad will call and tell you he's entered counseling, and he's beginning to realize some of the ways he failed you as a father?

Your dad is the same today as he's always been. You've tried to talk to him and nothing has worked. Is it reasonable to hope that he's going to change now? This is Nietzsche's point.

It seems foolish to hope Dad will change. It's like putting your head in the sand and *ignoring what your life has already taught you*. It's ignoring the data, ignoring the experiences you've amassed over twenty years of hoping in vain for your father to change. Isn't it more realistic to simply admit, "Dad's just not going to change. So stop *wanting* him to."

And there's the key—*wanting*. Hope is letting yourself want. And when you let yourself want something you do not have, you experience an inward groaning. You feel the longing. Your whole body fills with the ache of not-yet-met desire.

What is your relationship to your unmet desires ... right now? Reflecting on this will help you better understand your war with hope. What do you long for in this season of your life?

> A partner who is actually *for you*.
>
> Meaningful work.
>
> Your child to be healed of a disability.
>
> A parent who acknowledges how they harmed you.
>
> Your anxiety and fear to stop tormenting you.

Your cancer to go into remission.

A fulfilling and erotic sex life.

If you let yourself want—let yourself long for something—you are well on your way to hope. But you're not there yet. Hope also requires that you *wait expectantly.*

Hope is not merely longing for a spouse: it is longing for a spouse while, at the same time, expecting to meet them tonight. Groaning inwardly while waiting expectantly. That's hope.

Hope is both longing for a spouse and anticipating walking down the aisle.

Hope is both yearning for more intimacy with your partner and anticipating a romantic evening tonight.

Hope is both longing for more meaningful employment and envisioning yourself at your new job. *Anticipating it.*

Recall Psalm 27:13: "I remain confident of this: I will see the goodness of the Lord *in the land of the living*" (emphasis mine).

In the land of the living. In other words, I will see the goodness of the Lord in this life, before I die, before heaven. Can you feel in your body how agonizing it is to let yourself yearn for the specific things you want?

ALTERNATIVES TO HOPE

When hope feels too risky (or too stupid), we tend toward one of two alternative postures: (1) we deaden our desire (try to kill our longings), or (2) we resign ourselves to cynicism.

It's important to understand your body *naturally* yearns and groans. Look at children. They are a mass of longings. They always want something. In other words, groaning/longing/desiring is the natural disposition of the human heart. It's a good thing to desire something you don't yet have.

But when you let your body long for something and you don't get it, disappointment sets in.

Over time, these disappointments pile up. When they do so, you tend to become filled with doubt, questions about God, and anger (usually anger at yourself for *letting yourself want* in the first place).

When repeated disappointments make longing for something too painful, the tendency is to *kill your desire*. You think it is your enemy. *If I didn't want that thing so badly, I wouldn't hurt so much.* And so, slowly but surely, you try to deaden your desire, to numb it out.

Instead of hoping your spouse will begin pursuing your heart, you say to yourself, *They're just not like that, and besides, it's a broken world—maybe my expectations are too high.* What is that? It's a way of deadening your desire to be pursued by your spouse.

All deadening of desire springs from a hatred of hope. It's an attempt to manage the degree to which we are hoping God will come through. You wish you could stop hoping God would do the miraculous and create change in your spouse's heart.

"We're Done."

In Darren Aronofsky's film *The Wrestler*, character Randy Robinson has an estranged relationship with his adult daughter, Stephanie. It's clear from the beginning of the film that Randy and Stephanie are deeply alienated from each other, and that Stephanie carries years of hurt and anger. However, as the film unfolds, Randy moves to rebuild his relationship with his daughter. He confesses to her how he massively failed her as a father and how he wants to make that right. Stephanie begins to hope that there can be reconciliation. *She lets herself long for her father* to actually be a father again. They set up a time to go out to a restaurant and begin rebuilding what is so broken.

In the next scene, Stephanie is sitting alone in her house, devastated. Randy never showed up. She waited in the restaurant for two hours. Two hours. Imagine what she was feeling in her body as ten minutes became fifteen, which became fifty.

Later that evening, Randy knocks on her door. Stephanie starts screaming at him for not showing up. She screams about how what just happened is just like every other time in their relationship. There is only fury. But then you watch Stephanie experience a profound internal shift. She calms down . . . way down. She gets this cold, matter-of-fact look on her face. And with a calm and controlled voice, she looks her father right in the eye and simply says, "This relationship is broken—permanently. There's no fixing this."

And then she deadens all desire for a father as she says, "I don't want to see you. I don't want anything from you. We're done."[2]

Notice her words: "I don't *want* anything from you." It was too painful to want. Too painful to *desire* a father. So, she killed her desire. It was too painful to accept her dad's apology, set up another time to meet at the restaurant . . . and hope again that Dad would show up.

Deadening desire is saying, "I'm done wanting this thing." It's a way of trying to kill hope.

"I'm Not Cynical, I'm Realistic."

The second alternative to hope is resigning yourself to cynicism. Repeated disappointments can easily lead to cynicism. Instead of waiting expectantly for the letter that says you have been accepted into your first-choice school, cynicism says, *It's not going to happen*. Instead of starting some new endeavor—which would invite you to hope—you think to yourself, *That will never work*.

Cynicism is often fueled by the sentence, "I'm just being realistic."

---

2. *The Wrestler*, directed by Darren Aronofsky (Los Angeles: 20th Century Fox, 2009).

Consider speaking with a woman who longs for her husband to actually talk to her and care for her and pursue her heart. She's been asking him to do this for a decade, and very little has changed. As you are listening to her anguish, you name her war with hoping that her husband will change.

She responds to you by saying, "It's not that I lack hope, it's that I'm being realistic. Realistic about what I can expect from life in this world. It would be foolish to hope that my husband would really begin engaging my heart. We've fought about it for twenty years, and he hasn't done it yet. I'm not cynical, I'm realistic."

The part of us that has given itself over to cynicism is confident in its data-driven conclusion that hope is foolish. I get it. I feel this war frequently. But here's the dilemma: *there is nothing more unrealistic than the resurrection of Jesus Christ.*

If you are a Christian, *your entire life is based on something wildly unrealistic.*

If Jesus is resurrected, then there is no situation in your life that cannot be upended and reversed.

Christian Cynicism

There is a form of cynicism I call "Christian cynicism." There's nothing Christian about it, yet not only do many Christians embrace it but we also justify it with theology. Christian cynicism is fueled by sentences like "It's a broken world," and "I'm not going to get everything I long for until heaven."

Have you heard those sentences? Have you *spoken* those sentences? I sure have.

The dilemma with them is that they're true. It *is* a broken world. And our longings won't be fully met until heaven. However, we often use those sentences as a way to kill hope and to deaden desire. But that is utterly cynical.

It's cynicism bolstered by theology, yet it has nothing to do with Jesus. Why? Because it's a denial of the resurrection. Is it a broken world? Yes . . . but his broken body was resurrected. Will all your longings be met in this world? Of course not . . . *but you don't know which ones.*

And there's the rub. The question you have to wrestle with is, What can I hope for from God in the land of the living?

The psalmist claimed he would see God's goodness in the land of the living. When did you stop being able to say that? At what point in your story did it begin to seem foolish?

Barrenness as Hopelessness

The Bible is deeply honest about the reality of hopelessness in human life. The biblical metaphor for hopelessness is *barrenness*. Israel's story begins in barrenness. Sarah was barren—until she was an elderly woman! Rebecca and Rachel were also unable to have children. Sarah, Rebecca, and Rachel—the mothers of the first three generations of Israelites—were barren! What is the story of our origins telling us? Barrenness is fundamental to the experience of walking with God. Which is to say that all who follow Jesus inevitably have a war with hope.

Where is the barrenness in *your life* right now? Where do you feel powerless to create life and goodness and newness?

Who among us does not know something of the restless torment that comes from the war between the part of us that believes God actually cares about our longings and the part that looks around and sees all the evidence that God is not coming through for us?

Your war with hope is fueled by your awareness that *you don't know* which of your longings God will fulfill in this life. And you don't want to *wrestle* with God about meeting those desires. Herein lies the biggest reason we hate hope: *hope forces us to wrestle with God.*

Most wrestling with God is avoided by the simple phrase: "If it be your will." You risk expressing a desire to God—you ask for something specific—and then you tag on, "If it be your will."

"Not my will but yours be done" sounds so biblical. And indeed it is . . . as long as it comes *after* a twelve-round wrestling match with God.

You may be thinking, *Aren't we supposed to surrender our will to God's will?*

Yes, but that's just the point—you're called to *surrender* your will to God's will. Dan Allender points out that the word *surrender* implies there has *already been* a long, drawn out, bloody war. In other words, you *can't* surrender until you have fought with God. In war, you don't surrender until there is no hope left for accomplishing your objective and defeating the enemy. You fight until you have no strength left to fight any longer. Surrender only comes in a moment of exhaustion.

If you're not exhausted from fighting with God, then the words, "Not my will but yours be done" are not words of surrender; they are words you use to allow yourself to escape the agony of hoping.

THE PARABLE OF THE PERSISTENT WIDOW

In Luke 18, Jesus tells a fascinating parable about a widow who has gobs of hope. Specifically, she has hope that justice will be done to her adversary, the person who has harmed her. In the parable, the widow repeatedly goes to a judge with the plea, "Grant me justice against my adversary" (Luke 18:3). Since the widow keeps coming back to insist on the rightness of her case, the judge finally relents and grants her justice. Then Jesus says, "Will not God bring about justice for his chosen ones, who cry out to him day and night? Will he keep putting them off?" (v. 7).

The first thing to notice about this parable is that it's not called "the Parable of the Widow Who Surrendered to God's Will." *The whole point is that she refused to take no for an answer.*

She knew nothing of "Maybe it's not God's will for me to get justice in this life."

Until you take the risk of hoping that God will fulfill the desires of your heart in this life—until you bring your disappointment and anger to God—God will always remain strangely impersonal to you. You might know God as the Savior of the world, but you won't know God as who the psalmist calls *the God of My Rescue.*[3]

Hope is agonizing because it requires us to hold both death *and* resurrection. Most of us focus on either death *or* resurrection. But if we open our eyes to what's actually happening in the world, life is filled with many deaths and many resurrections. We are called to be honest about both.

To live into both.

To feel both.

Deeply.

This is why Paul says we are to rejoice with those who rejoice and mourn with those who mourn.

Many of us think hopeful people are those who always see the resurrections in the world. They always see the good things happening. Dan Allender is fond of saying that if you are focused *solely* on resurrection, you are not a hopeful person—you're an optimistic person.

Hope has nothing to do with optimism.

---

[3]. "Lead me in Your truth and instruct me, for You are the God of my rescue" (Ps. 25:5). Robert Alter, *The Book of Psalms: A Translation with Commentary* (New York: W. W. Norton, 2009), 85.

Optimism is a denial of the darkness that permeates the world, and it requires closing your eyes to the tragedies and injustices on every corner. Do you close your eyes to the heartaches that have happened to you? To the wrongs that are currently happening to others—especially those who are being marginalized and oppressed?

We do not live this both/and well. It is far easier to live either/or.

You may focus on the darkness of this world but have a hard time seeing the thousands of places where the Spirit of God is doing beautiful, redemptive things. Or perhaps you focus on the beauty in this world but turn a blind eye to all the desperation and despair right in front of you. The Spirit of God calls us to see both. In full color.

A life of both/and means you are just as apt to be weeping one moment as you are to be laughing the next. You are never far from mourning (because you have eyes wide open to the pain in this world) and never far from rejoicing (because you have eyes wide open to the goodness of God in the land of the living).

The Hope You Already Have

How much hope do you have? You likely have significantly more than you realize. You may not be fond of it, but will you have the integrity to confess how much hope you actually still have?

Think of all the disappointments you've endured in your life. Think of all the prayers you've prayed, all the times you've cried out to God and have not seen God come through for you in the way you wanted. And yet you're still interested in God, still talking to God, still pursuing God. You haven't given up on God. God matters to you.

Indeed, you understand Nietzsche's argument all too well. You want healing in some area of your life, and you've pleaded with God . . . and the healing has not yet come. That's tormenting. How do you understand why you continue believing in God, praying to God, pleading with God? How do you understand why a significant part of you still believes God is benevolent and, in some real way, *for you*? Nietzsche calls this foolishness; the Bible calls it hope.

Is It Reasonable to Hope?

In Jeremiah 30:12, God says to Israel: "Your wound is incurable, your injury beyond healing."

This is precisely the *felt sense* of many people with a history of trauma. We feel as if we have an incurable wound.

Is there an area of your life that seems too broken to be healed?

Just a few verses later, God says something new: "But I will restore you to health and heal your wounds" (v. 17).

> In verse 12 God says, "Your wound is incurable, your injury beyond healing."
>
> In verse 17, God says, "But I will restore you to health and heal your wounds."

Now, which is it? Either your wound is incurable and therefore cannot be healed, *or* God can heal your wound, which means it wasn't incurable in the first place.

This text holds together two truths that seem incompatible: we can have an incurable wound *and* that wound can be cured.

Do you feel like some of your wounds are incurable? Do you sometimes feel like your injured heart is too damaged for genuine healing to occur?

Jeremiah 30 is vitally important for people who have a history of trauma.

Why? Because these verses acknowledge two things that seem to be impossible to hold together. On the one hand, the text acknowledges the severity of the wound, and on the other hand, the text acknowledges the possibility of healing.

In other words, God does not deny the severity of your wound (*it is incurable*). But, at the same time, *God will heal what cannot be healed.*

This paradox is difficult for most modern people to understand because we have lost touch with the category of *promise*.

Do you believe the promise of God is a *reasonable* category? Do you believe it is reasonable to trust in the promise of God to create newness in your life when all you can see is your incurable wound?

You and I are living in the twenty-first century, which means we are children of the Enlightenment, which occurred in the late seventeenth and eighteenth centuries. Before this time, people had a much more magical view of the world. But the Enlightenment came along and said, "What is possible can only spring from what humans can do *by themselves*." As a result, promise ceased to be a viable intellectual category.

In other words, we trained our imaginations to stop being able to conceive of God intervening in a hopeless situation and creating something genuinely new out of that hopeless situation. The philosophy of the Enlightenment shrunk the human imagination to only consider those things we human beings could make or create on our own.

Do you have space in your imagination for something new to happen in your life not because you make it happen but because Someone Other Than You creates it?

The kingdom of evil is committed to shrinking our imagination so that the best we can envision is a rearrangement of the existing pieces of our lives. We have lost an imagination *for the genuinely new*.

But think about this for a minute. What is required for the genuinely new to come into existence in your life? An act of *creation*.

Most of us believe in a Creator. Do we think the Creator stopped making new things after the big bang? What if the Creator has the freedom to *continue* to create new things?

The present ordering of your life—the way things are currently—claims to be the final ordering of your life. But what if the Creator is free to create new green shoots in your life that are *underived* from your present circumstances?

As you are reading this, can you feel your imagination open to this possibility? Can you feel hope rise? And then can you feel something inside of you slam the door shut on that rising hope? It's the little voice of *Don't be a fool; you've hoped in the past and it's only led to disappointment.*

Why is hope reasonable? Because the history of the world is the history of a Maker making new things that are underived from the present circumstances.

First, God spoke to the darkness of chaos and, in God's freedom to speak, a new world came into existence. Creation, in other words, is *intrinsic* to the way things are in this world. Creation is the way this whole thing started. God spoke newness, and behold—there was an expanding universe.

Second, God spoke to barren Sarah and, in God's freedom to speak, a new family came into existence. And God's words to Abraham and Sarah were spoken against all the data and all the evidence. The birth of Isaac was not derived from the present ordering of things, which was that Abraham and Sarah were too old to conceive a child.

Third, God spoke to oppressed slaves in Egypt and, in God's freedom to speak, a new community of people came into existence. The present ordering of things was slavery, until the people cried out to God and God responded with yet another act of creation (deliverance from slavery).[4]

We all war with hope. However, the nature of that war looks different for each of us. What are two or three things you are afraid to

---

4. As with so much in this chapter, I am deeply indebted to Walter Brueggemann for identifying these three acts of creation. See Brueggemann, *Prophetic Imagination*.

hope for? What would it feel like to write down those two or three things? Use the space below to do so.

Of equal importance, what is something you have stopped hoping for? Perhaps you once had hope for this thing, but somewhere along the way it became too painful to continue hoping, and so you stopped.

CHAPTER 12 **KEY POINTS**

- Engaging your story can be a daunting journey, especially when it involves confronting the spectrum of hope and hopelessness.
- Your war with hope is fueled by your awareness that you don't know which of your longings God will fulfill in this life.
- Hope is a delicate balance between longing and waiting, between anticipation and uncertainty. It's a paradoxical force that both sustains us and torments us, pushing us to yearn for what seems unattainable while daring us to believe in the possibility of transformation.

13

WHAT IF YOU DIDN'T HAVE TO DO THIS ALONE?

> A story that has not been shared communally is a story that has you bound in shame.
>
> Dan Allender

You were created to need.

You were created to need *other people*.

This is God's fault. God made you needy. This was true when you were three days old. It was equally true when you were thirteen years old. And it is just as true today. God made you to need other human beings.

Neuroscientist Stephen Porges asserts that "connection is a biological imperative."[1] His point is that if you don't have sufficient

---

1. As quoted in Bonnie Badenoch, "Becoming a Therapeutic Presence in the Counseling Room and the World," in *Interpersonal Neurobiology and Clinical Practice*, ed. by Daniel J. Siegel, Allan N. Schore, and Louis Cozolino, Norton Series on Interpersonal Neurobiology (New York: W. W. Norton, 2021), 133.

connection with other human beings, you will become a little bit less alive each day. Your biology—your body—*needs* emotional connection with other people to flourish and thrive. Dr. Bonnie Badenoch puts it like this: all human beings have a "genetically embedded need for connection."[2]

Skin is significantly overrated as a barrier.

Most people think they are physically separate from those around them because of skin. This is not the case.

From a neurobiological perspective, it is more accurate to say that you and I exist "within each other" rather than apart from each other.

When two people are in proximity, their respective nervous systems are deeply intertwined. According to neuroscience, it is not a stretch to say that "there is no 'me' apart from 'us.'"[3] The reason relationships are so crucial for life (and healing) is because your brain exists as much *between you and another person* as it exists within you. As Dan Siegel says, the most neurobiologically accurate pronoun to describe the human experience is neither *me* nor *we* but *mwe*.[4]

Siegel's point is that you and I are not separate from each other.

This "genetically embedded need for connection" may feel like a deeply inconvenient truth, especially if you lack close relationships. But it's a truth that, if aligned with, can guide you into significant healing.

It's important to understand that you cannot adequately engage your story alone. Sitting in your favorite chair with a journal, a Bible, a cup of coffee, and a good view out your window is not sufficient to heal your wounds.

You cannot uncover the truth of the most pivotal stories of your life *by yourself*.

---

2. Badenoch, "Becoming a Therapeutic Presence," 119.
3. Badenoch, "Becoming a Therapeutic Presence," 116.
4. Siegel, *IntraConnected*.

Moreover, adding God to the mix is also insufficient. You cannot engage your story merely with God's help and God's presence. Why? Because you were made to need other people. Again, this is God's fault. It's the natural by-product of being created in the image of The Relationship. In God's humility, God created human beings to need more than Godself. God made our brains and nervous systems to need *one another*. And this is particularly true when it comes to healing from wounds.

If you asked the apostle Paul, "Where is the resurrected Christ?" Paul would not have pointed at the heavens. He would have pointed at other Christians. For Paul, the resurrected Christ was visibly present in other believers—that is, in the *body* of Christ.

The resurrected Christ is alive on planet Earth—living in and through other human beings.

Here's the really good news: when your nervous system is sufficiently supported by another settled, wise nervous system (another human being offering witness and presence), then your nervous system will heal.

In neurobiological terms, healing equals *neural integration*. An integrated brain is a healed brain. Here's how Badenoch explains the necessary supportive conditions for healing to occur:

> While the capacity for neural integration is built into our system, *it requires the presence of another to emerge*. . . . We relational people are full of inherent capacities that blossom through nourishing connection with another. This means that our system's healing capacity is *innate and ongoing*, needing only the accompaniment of someone who can enter with us into the vulnerable places that hold our traumas.[5]

Your wounds will heal naturally when the environment is right. The right environment for healing is the empathic presence of another person.

---

5. Badenoch, "Becoming a Therapeutic Presence," 120. Emphasis mine.

What if there were people out there who could help you explore your story? What if there were people who would truly listen to you, validate your experiences, and provide an empathic witness to the core stories of your life? Your life will only make sense after it has been witnessed by another.

As a therapist, the most healing thing I do for my clients is *bear witness* to their stories.

The opposite of trauma is not "no trauma." **The opposite of trauma is connection.** Bad events only turn into embedded traumas when there is no witness to offer connection and care.

It doesn't matter how awful the experience was; if you have a loving, compassionate, empathic witness you can run home to and process your feelings with and receive comfort from, the awful experience will not become an embedded trauma that you carry inside your body. We are all very resilient when we have access to sufficient care and support.

Suppose you were molested by your grandfather as a girl. Decades later you share a little bit about the story with your Bible study group. Instead of validating your experience, naming you well in the experience, and offering genuine presence, comfort, and engagement, your group spiritualizes away the trauma and dismisses your pain. You'll leave the group thinking, *I just can't recover from my grandfather molesting me.* The reality is that it's not your grandfather who is keeping you stuck; it's the emotional immaturity of your Bible study group. It's the group's unwillingness to enter into your pain and bear witness to what you suffered as a girl.

DO I REALLY HAVE TO SHARE MY STORY WITH ANOTHER PERSON?

Tragically, many of us live in one of the most individualistic cultures in history. As a result, it's common for people to ask, "Do I really have to share my story with another person? Can't I just do this by myself?" The answer is, "No, you can't engage your story by yourself." You absolutely have to tell your story to another person and experience their engagement of your story. There are at least three reasons for this.

First, in order to heal, you need to experience what's called *limbic resonance*. This is a fancy way of saying that your brain needs to experience someone attuning to you and empathizing with your big emotions. Dan Siegel calls this experience "feeling felt."[6] You cannot feel felt by yourself. You feel felt when another person truly listens to one of your stories. In this moment, an *interpersonal joining* happens. It is this interpersonal joining that creates the environment for the brain and body to heal naturally. When we are joined by another and feel felt, our wounds begin to heal all by themselves.

It's hard to overstate the importance of being understood and validated when it comes to healing from past harm. The more deeply you feel a particular emotion, the greater your need to be understood in that moment. It is very vulnerable to risk sharing big feelings. This is because if we are not interpersonally joined when we share intense feelings, we will feel high levels of shame.[7] But if we have limbic resonance with another person who connects with us, the experience of being joined by that person creates significant healing in the brain.

Second, in order to heal, you need to feel your unfelt feelings from the past. And you can't feel these *by yourself*. Why? Because these feelings are inherently dysregulating. Recall that nothing healing can happen when your brain/body is in a state of dysregulation.

It is the interpersonal joining with another person that allows your nervous system to stay regulated enough to feel your big unfelt

---

6. Siegel and Hartzel, *Parenting from the Inside Out*.
7. Daniel Siegel, *The Developing Mind: Toward a Neurobiology of Interpersonal Experience* (New York: Guilford Press, 1999), 335.

feelings from the past. If another person is fully present with you when you become dysregulated, the resonance circuitry in your brain will allow you to mirror their settled, regulated presence. When this happens, your body will begin to regulate.[8]

Siegel puts it this way:

> Here is a key fact about relationships: the resonance circuitry not only allows us to "feel felt" and to connect with one another, but it also helps to regulate our internal state. In other words, the interpersonal resonance between [my client] and me could help her ... feel safe enough to feel her own feelings. This is how in the moment, face-to-face interactions initiate long-term synaptic changes.[9]

When the presence of another wise, kind guide creates an environment in which you can feel your unfelt feelings from the past, your brain will heal as these fragmented neural networks (unfelt feelings) are integrated.

A third reason you need another human being to experience healing is that healing requires the accurate co-construction of your autobiographical narrative. In other words, your story needs to make sense to you. This inevitably requires the outside perspective of another person. Each of us is way too close to our own story to see it accurately and, therefore, tell it coherently. In order for your story to make sense, all the characters in your story—including you—need to be named well. By "named well" I mean that each character's dignity and depravity must be clearly articulated. The temptation, of course, is to sugarcoat the darkness of pivotal actors in the most formative stories of your life.

Until the key characters in your story are named well, you will not be able to fully access your unfelt feelings from the past.

---

8. In addition, you will begin to build neural networks that allow for increased self-regulation in the future! See Daniel J. Siegel, *Mindsight: The New Science of Personal Transformation* (New York: Bantam Books, 2010), chapter 7.

9. Siegel, *Mindsight*, 138–39.

The nature of trauma is that the story can't be told; it is too overwhelming to feel, to know, to tell. However, when another wise and courageous person speaks into your story and names truth truthfully, then—together—the two of you are able to arrive at a more accurate and coherent telling of what actually happened.

In his important book, *The Neuroscience of Psychotherapy*, Louis Cozolino explains that the co-construction of narratives is necessary for healing. His primary point is that when you finally arrive at a truthful telling of what happened to you, your brain is able to integrate neural networks that were previously disconnected due to a traumatic (inaccurate) telling of the story. "In editing our narratives, we change the organization and nature of our memories and, hence, reorganize our brains."[10]

The brain heals its own wounds to the degree that it reorganizes around the truth of your stories. Said another way, healing from trauma is all about the continual endeavor to tell your story more truthfully, which necessarily requires an attuned and caring witness. In the words of bell hooks, "Rarely, if ever, are any of us healed in isolation."[11]

ENGAGE AND CONNECT

The process of reflecting on your story, sharing your story with another person, and hearing that person's reaction to your story *connects* neural networks that were previously separated.

As a result of trauma, the various regions of your brain become disconnected from one another. In particular, trauma impairs integration between the left and right hemispheres of your brain and

---

10. Louis Cozolino, *The Neuroscience of Psychotherapy: Healing the Social Brain*, 2nd ed., Norton Series on Interpersonal Neurobiology (New York: W. W. Norton, 2010), 92.
11. bell hooks, *All About Love: New Visions* (New York: William Morrow, 2000), 215.

between the "top" (cortical) and "bottom" (limbic) areas of your brain. The more integrated your brain, the more healthy and stable you are. When another wise, settled nervous system engages your story with you, the emotional presence of that person allows you to feel unfelt feelings in your brain and put words to those feelings. When that happens, connectivity in your brain increases in two primary ways:

1. The left and right hemispheres of your brain become more deeply connected.
2. Your prefrontal cortex becomes more deeply connected with the limbic portions of your brain.

Both of the above are very healing for your brain.

Here's the point: *the presence of an attuned listener leads to changes in your brain.*

The single most important key to healing is *connecting*. Connecting with another person's attuned presence, connecting with your physical body from the neck down, connecting neural networks in your brain that are separated from one another, connecting with God.

The new field of interpersonal neurobiology demonstrates that the key to connecting previously fragmented neural networks is the attuned and caring presence of another human being. Trauma therapist Resmaa Menakem says that sharing your story with another person means

> describing an event that had meaning for you, while the other person listens with caring, full attention, a calm presence, and a settled body. This might involve both of you letting you tremble, cry, sway, shake your head, or move your body in some other way as it metabolizes the experience.[12]

---

12. Menakem, *My Grandmother's Hands*, 177.

THE VILLAGE

In Francis Weller's book *The Wild Edge of Sorrow*, he points out that most modern people are "waiting for the village to appear."[13] The "village" refers to a few other people who have these characteristics:

1. They care deeply about your growth, maturation, and healing.
2. They are more mature than you and stronger than you (they've done their own work of healing and transformation).
3. They are eager to respond to you by providing comfort, care, and guidance.
4. They are willing to make themselves available to you when you need them.

That's the village! Can you imagine if you had two or three people who fit that description?

Weller argues that when we come into the world, we are designed to anticipate the presence of the village.[14] In other words, we are created to expect that there will be at least two or three other people in our lives who meet the above four criteria.

And we are created to expect that *these people will always be there for us.*

If the village is not there for us as we grow up, we begin to isolate, believing we are on our own to figure out life and figure out healing.

When the village is absent, there is no way to feel a sense of belonging. We might gain acceptance to some inner ring, but true belonging evades us. This is because true belonging comes from knowing in the depth of our being that the village is there for us.

---

13. Francis Weller, *The Wild Edge of Sorrow: Rituals of Renewal and the Sacred Work of Grief* (Berkeley: North Atlantic Books, 2015), 54.
14. Weller, *Wild Edge of Sorrow*, 55.

The village is another way of speaking about *elders*. Most modern cultures lack elders. An "elder" is simply someone who knows how to handle their power. Elders are warrior kings and queens who know that (a) they have power, and (b) their power is intended to be used on behalf of the community, particularly on behalf of the wounded.

Weller suggests that most of us are "waiting for the village to appear so we can fully acknowledge our sorrows."[15] I would extend this to say that we are waiting for the village to appear so we can fully acknowledge all of our emotions and fully tell all of our stories.

We are waiting for the village to appear so we can risk speaking candidly about our struggles and pain. If no one is there to help us heal, why would we risk speaking honestly about our great hurts? *But*, consider this invitation from Weller:

> Imagine the feeling of relief that would flood our whole being if we knew that when we were in the grip of sorrow, our village would respond to our need.[16]

How relieved would you be if you knew in your gut that anytime you needed comfort, care, or guidance, the village would show up immediately and help you through the hard things?

What if you didn't have to figure out healing by yourself?

Now, I know all too well that the village is hard to find. Sometimes it feels impossible to find. What matters most is that you persist in looking. This may mean ending unhealthy relationships and finding new ones. In short, you need to keep doing whatever you can think of to find or develop a small community of like-minded warriors to help you engage your story. Grit and persistence will take you further than you might imagine.

---

15. Weller, *Wild Edge of Sorrow*, 54.
16. Weller, *Wild Edge of Sorrow*, 72.

When it comes to sharing your story, avoid these two extremes: telling no one and telling everyone. By *everyone* I mean "everyone who will listen regardless of whether or not they have earned the right to hear your story."

It's important to be judicious about who you give editorial privilege over your life. Which voices do you respect enough to give their words weight? Who in your life deserves to have editorial privilege in your heart? This list should be short. Very short. Sadly, most of us are not in relationship with many people who have earned the right to speak into our lives.

NEXT STEPS

I hope I've stressed the necessity of exploring your story *with someone else*—namely, a trained, wise guide.

I know some (not many) coaches and story consultants who are more skilled than licensed therapists in guiding you through the process of engaging your story. The credentials of LCSW or LPC or PhD tell me nothing about a particular therapist's skill level. They tell me the person made it through graduate school. Period. That's it. The ability to understand attachment theory or interpersonal neurobiology or affect regulation does not make someone worthy of hearing your story.

So, how do you find someone to help you engage your story?

A good place to start is word of mouth. If you have a friend who is working with someone, and you notice that your friend is growing and maturing, find out who they are working with. Contact that person and interview them. Ask these questions:

- What have you done to engage your own story in the last three years?
- Do you receive regular video supervision/consultation, and if so, from whom?

> How will your understanding of trauma inform your work with me?

Remember that you can always switch therapists. This is not failure on your part, and not necessarily failure on the therapist's part.

FINAL WORD

Good books are full of good information. The dilemma is that information does not change the human heart. What changes the human heart is engaging your story—with kindness and *with others*.

Let me say that again: what changes the human heart is engaging your story . . . with kindness . . . and with others.

Engaging your story is not going to make all your pain go away. However, it will lead to genuine healing. And, more importantly, engaging your story will bring rest to your body. There is a rest in finally understanding why you are the way you are. Why you behave the way you behave. Why you feel the way you feel. There is profound rest that comes with finally understanding these things. At last, your life makes sense.

ACKNOWLEDGMENTS

To include Dan Allender in my acknowledgments is like Steve Kerr acknowledging Michael Jordan for his role on the Chicago Bulls. Nothing in this book would exist without Dan's prophetic eyes and courageous tongue. Dan, you are one of the most humble men I know, and one of the few warriors left. Every life I touch is your fruit.

Thank you to my agent, Andrea Heinecke—throughout the process, you have been an advocate for my voice to come through.

Thank you to Stephanie Smith, my editor—you both made the writing better and protected me from publishing sentences that simply were not true.

Thank you to my early readers: Mandy Hughes, Janet Stark, Lora Kelley, Kate Chittenden, Jason Faulkner, Susan Tucker, and Carrie Ott.

Thank you to Rick Wilson, John Depasquale, and Brian Glenny—you each met with me in a different season of heartache and pain. I can say without hyperbole that each of you saved my life.

I don't know how to sufficiently express gratitude to Andy Ide, my therapist for ten years. More than anyone else, you brought attunement and containment when my world was in crisis.

Thank you to KJ Ramsey. I still remember when you said to me, "Adam, this book is not the definitive word on the subject, but it is an offering of goodness." That sentence freed me to begin writing.

Thank you to Jen Oyama Murphy and Rebecca Wheeler Walston—you both were exceedingly gracious in helping me tone down the chapter on engaging our collective story. May the day come when this is no longer necessary.

Thank you to Rob Bell—your audiobook *Something to Write* moved me times without number to continue creating.

Thank you to all the listeners of *The Place We Find Ourselves* podcast. I wrote this book for you.

Thank you to my wife, Caroline, for pointing out all the places where my writing was less than clear (or simply inaccurate).

Thank you to my daughter, Hope—the power of your presence is as fierce as it is lovely.

Thank you to my son, Eli—your sensitivity and compassion make me want to be a better man.

Finally, thank you to my twin brothers, Jacob and Jason. You are the only two people who really know what happened.

ADAM YOUNG is a trauma therapist and the host of *The Place We Find Ourselves* podcast. He is a Licensed Clinical Social Worker (LCSW) with master's degrees in social work (Virginia Commonwealth University) and divinity (Emory University). Adam regularly speaks at conferences and serves as a fellow with The Allender Center. He lives in Fort Collins, Colorado, with his wife and two children.

CONNECT WITH ADAM:

- AdamYoungCounseling.com
- AdamYoung and AdamYoungCounseling
- @AdamYoungCounseling
- @AdamYoungCounseling361